Going Deeper
A 30-Day Devotional

Pastor Frank & Samuel Gervasi

MIDWEST CHRISTIAN PUBLISHING

ISBN: 979-8-218-64488-8

Going Deeper – A 30-Day Devotional

Going Deeper – A 30-Day Devotional

__In Dedication:__ Written and dedicated to Rosetta Gervasi. A truly kind & generous spirit who embraced the Cross fully in an I.C.U room before being called home. You are greatly missed! We look forward to the day we will see you again...

Going Deeper – A 30-Day Devotional

Introduction:

Whether you are someone who has a good walk with the Lord or just wanting to draw closer to Christ. Every person of faith finds themselves wanting or needing of a better connection with God. For the person who has drifted, we don't always remember how it happened or how we arrived at that point in our spiritual journey. However, we are all at one time or another, awakened by the realization that we want more of God.

We remember as David did in the Psalms, times where we enjoyed our relationship and our closeness with God. He says, *"These things I remember as I pour out my soul: how I used to go to the house of God under the protection of the Mighty One with shouts of joy and praise among the festive throng." (Psalm 42:4, NIV)* So, we make the decision and commitment to grow in our faith and press hard after God once again. To experience the thriving faith that we want for ourselves.

Our hope and prayer are that you take these next thirty days with the ***Going Deeper Devotion*** and be purposeful in pressing hard after God through these reflections. Each day has a passage that will help the reader be reminded of God's Faithfulness and goodness. The ***Big Idea*** for that reflection and passage giving the main point or permanent principle. An *expanded* take-away thought in the ***Insight*** section. Along with a daily ***Challenge*** and ***Prayer*** sections to solidify the reflection and growth for that respective devotion. Additionally, each devotion includes a ***Going Deeper*** section that features some writer, commentator, or expanded reference for the day's passage or ideas.

We hope you faithfully use and enjoy the ***Going Deeper Devotional.***

Going Deeper – A 30-Day Devotional

Going Deeper – A 30-Day Devotional

Going Deeper
A 30-Day Devotional
by Pastor Frank and Samuel Gervasi

Table of Contents:

Going Deeper – A 30-Day Devotional

#1 - Crowning of the King
Read: *Luke 19:35-40*

"I tell you, He replied, 'If they keep quiet the stones will cry out.'" **Luke 19:40, NIV**

Every day, when the sun rises over Washington, D.C., it's light first falls on the eastern side of the city's tallest structure, the 555-foot Washington Monument. The first part of this historic monument is to reflect the rising Sun is the eastern side of its aluminum capstone, where one will see the Latin words inscribed, *Laus Deo,* which when translated into English reads, *"Praise be to God."*

Praise is one of the most discussed topics in scripture. In fact, our reading today probably shows one of the greatest moments of worship that Christ experiences on this side of heaven. In our passage, we see the people exalt Christ as King as He rides triumphantly into Jerusalem and give Him the worship He's due. *1*

---

*Big Idea: **Always be prepared to worship Jesus –and honor Him –as the only true king.***

John MacArthur calls this passage, *"the Coronation of the King," 2* and references it as Christ's last public appearance before His crucifixion. Which I think is an appropriate title for this passage, because it sounds more regal, like a ceremony for royalty. And this is exactly the reason the people of Jerusalem are worshipping with such joy. In v. 37 it says, *"When he came near the place where the road goes down the Mount of Olives, the whole crowd of disciples began joyfully to praise God in loud voices for all the miracles they had seen."* It was finally time!

Going Deeper – A 30-Day Devotional

Consider how they had been hearing about the coming Messiah for so many years throughout the Old Testament readings in the various synagogues. Week after week! Year after year! Reading after reading! They had realized something important: that Jesus was the only true King, worthy of our worship and obedience. And we too need to understand this because how we view Christ and worshipping Him can make a difference.

Insight: Christ being King should mean that a person worships Christ in reverence. However, it also means that after we submit our life to Him, --that we live in ways that are consistent with His teachings.

See, the crowd understood that this was a big deal for these people and the time had arrived. They worship Him with their whole heart!

Challenge: What is my general mindset towards praise? Is it like in the passage? How can I improve my outlook on praise?

Pray: Asking God to help us have the same mindset...

Going Deeper:

In this passage, you may notice that Jesus comes into Jerusalem on what some Gospels describe as a *"donkey."* However, Matthew includes the word *foal"* which means that this donkey had never been ridden before. This donkey was one that was supposed to be for the coming Messiah. When Christ did this, He was fulfilling prophecy found in Zechariah 9:9, where it says, *"Rejoice greatly, daughter Zion! Shout, Daughter Jerusalem! See, you King comes to you, righteous and victorious, lowly and riding on a donkey, on a colt, the foal of a donkey."* 3

Devotion written by Pastor Frank & Samuel Gervasi

---

1. Wikipedia, https://en.wikipedia.org/wiki/Washington_Monument, as accessed on 11/03/2024.
2. Grace to You, https://www.gty.org/library/sermons-library/81-42/the-humble-coronation-of-king-jesus, as accessed on 11/03/2024.
3. New International Bible, Holy Bible, New International Version®, NIV® Copyright ©1973, 1978, 1984, 2011 by Biblica, Inc.® Used by permission. All rights reserved worldwide.

Going Deeper – A 30-Day Devotional

#2 - Membership is Not a Country Club
Read: *Ephesians 2:19-22*

"Consequently, you are no longer foreigners and strangers, but fellow citizens with God's people and also members of his household.'" **Ephesians 2:19, NIV**

Church membership has been said by some to be a very valuable tool for growing in faith. However, it really has been a misunderstood topic in many churches and believers across the country. In fact, it was recently reported that church membership has gone down 19% in the last sixteen years. Which is really a big number that has ramifications for the Spiritual maturity of many people, including the ones that were not part of this research.

Big Idea: *Christians become a part of a bigger family, and believers are growing and becoming a Holy Temple where God's Spirit Dwells.*

The apostle Paul when addressing the church at Ephesus wasn't necessarily correcting any bad or erroneous behaviors, or interpersonal issues with anyone. Rather he was giving, in part, a sound model for the type of relationships that should exist after a person becomes a Christ follower. In verse 19 he describes being, "members of Christ's household." Even though he may have been referring to Gentiles being included into God's family, he is also saying that we are *part "of a family with Christ as the head." 2* (verse 20.)

Insight: *Membership is a tool that God uses to grow each member into a family. Built on the principles of the Apostles with Christ as the Chief Cornerstone. Membership is a covenant between individual believers and a local church of commitment, where individuals and churches grow into a place where Christ's Spirit dwells.*

_____

Many times, people think that Church membership is not in the Bible. However, the concept is woven through the New Testament and one of the most important tools that God uses to grow us and His church. Now, the word itself (membership) is not found many times in that form. Nevertheless, in the book of Acts alone, approximately 82% of the passages regarding becoming a Christian are referring to the local body of believers and NOT the Universal Christian Church. There are approximately 17 references to where a person was added to the church. About 14 out of the 17 are giving an image of believers becoming part of a local congregation. That's not counting the epistles where the concept is also being modelled in the context of the local church. Obviously, it shows the importance of being connected to each other through a local body of believers.

Family relationships are always growing and changing over time. However, ultimately, we become a place where Christ's Spirit can dwell. Verse 29 says that, _"we are becoming a holy temple for the Lord."_ **1**

_____

Challenge: **_What mindsets get in the way of being a good member of my local church? What ways can I grow in the areas I serve? What ways could hinder God's Spirit dwelling in me?_**

Pray: **_Asking God to make my life a place where His Spirit would want to dwell....._**

_____

Going Deeper:

Member, even though the Greek word is not found in the New Testament. The concept of it is an important one and word. In the Old Testament it may not have been as imperative because Jewish life was centered around the Synagogue. They studied, went to school, served, and were instructed in the Torah. So, the idea of community was almost expected and just assumed. However, in the New Testament the concept of Membership became very important because the church was a new concept. As well as conflict that arose between orthodox Jews and the Christian Church. In fact, some of _"the times that the word is used in the New Testament refers to the organs of a body, as well as a part of the whole."_ (J. Knox, An Interpreter's Dictionary of the Bible, Abington Press, Copyright 1962.) _Especially in places_ like Matthew 5:29, Romans 6:13, Romans 7:23, Romans 12:4, and 1 Corinthians 12:12-27. Which is important because Christ viewed the church as members of a body intricately connected to Himself. _Membership is a_

Going Deeper – A 30-Day Devotional

covenant between individual believers and a local church of commitment, where individuals and churches grow into a place where Christ's Spirit dwells. 2

_____

Devotion written by Pastor Frank & Samuel Gervasi

_____

1. New International Version (NIV), Holy Bible, New International Version®, NIV® Copyright ©1973, 1978, 1984, 2011 by Biblica, Inc.® Used by permission. All rights reserved worldwide.
2. J. Knox, An Interpreter's Dictionary of the Bible, Abington Press, Copyright 1962.

Going Deeper – A 30-Day Devotional

#3 - Benefits of Strong Faith
Read: *John 4:46-54*

_____

"The Royal Official said, 'Sir, come down before my child dies.' 'Go,' Jesus replied, 'your son will live.'" **John 4:49-50, NIV**

_____

The dictionary defines faith as: *"the ability to trust in the worth or ability of someone or something." 1* However, it really is a great definition even though it's a secular one. Because it relates to matters of faith as well. Both in the concepts of belief in God ----*Himself*, and also belief in what the Scriptures tell us as well. Now, in the case of having trust in God, a person needs to accept who He says He is, *fully and completely*. Additionally, though it's also true because a person has to believe completely how the Bible commands, encourages, and exhorts us to live. Nevertheless, *that's not such an easy thing to do sometimes, is it?* Especially when you think about all the variables that come into play with life at times. Nevertheless, faith is a key ingredient needed for maximum growth regardless of how long a person has been walking with Christ.

_____

Big Idea: *Faith is required for all the seasons of a Christ-follower's life* **if** *they want to experience God's best in life.*

_____

Faith in *God* **and** His *abilities* is required for **all** of the Christian life, from beginning to end. For both *young* and *old*, both *small* and *big*, -for the newly saved to those who've been following Christ for several years. As well as, from the *smallest* thing, ---to the *biggest* thing we really need God for everything.

Going Deeper – A 30-Day Devotional

If you look at the context of the passage it was very simply for the healing of the Royal Official's son. Even though it doesn't tell us *what* the sickness was, it was definitely a *serious issue* because it says he was *"close to death." (v.47.)*

And, what's clear is that the official believed **fully** that Jesus could do the miraculous in his son's life. Because v. 47 says *"He went and begged"* **2** Christ for healing. Now, it could have been out of *desperation*, but most likely, it was because he had heard and maybe even seen second hand about all Christ had been doing. The miracles performed, the teaching with authority, and even challenging long held beliefs of the leaders of that day and culture.

———————

Insight: *Belief is really required for all needs in the Christian life. If you have a need, trust fully that God can do whatever is needed for you. Whether it's a minor relationship issue, are facing a major decision, or are at the receiving end of a major health scare.*

———————

Even Though God *Cares* About *Everything*—Christ's *First* Concern is a Person's *Soul.* Consider that, because He doesn't care more about your *health* than your final destination. He doesn't care about your *wealth* more than your soul. And He doesn't care about your *relationships* more than the place in eternity either! What Jesus **does** care about *most* is whether you've come to a place of repentance, and whether you've received the forgiveness that comes from embracing the Cross. (John 3:16.)

In verse 48 it *says "'Unless you people see signs and wonders,' Jesus told him, 'You will never believe.'"* **2** Even though Christ doesn't say that specifically, that is what was being referred to. Because the *signs and wonders* that people would see, were just the signs that He was the Son of God, that was to come into the World. The Kingdom of God had finally arrived.

Elizabeth Elliott, the missionary's wife who was killed by the Auca Indians that her husband was bringing the Gospel to, said this about belief: *"If you believe in a God who controls the big things, you must believe in God who controls the little things. It is we of course to whom things look little or big."* **3**

———————

Challenge: *What is my level of faith currently? Do I still believe God completely at His word, or not? How can I continue to grow in faith?*

Going Deeper – A 30-Day Devotional

<u>**Pray:**</u>   *Asking God to stretch my faith in Him, so that I can experience Him in a greater way....*

<u>*Going Deeper:*</u>

There's also another reason that shows the Royal Official had great faith. And that is, *because* he was said to have worked for Herod Antipas, the son of Herod the Great. Even though that doesn't sound like it's significant.it really is! Because he was *most likely* **not** very fond of Christ ---being raised around all that *jealously and animosity* towards Christ. In fact, Pilate sent Christ back to Antipas, and he was mocked and sent back and forth. So, the Royal Official that was asking for a miracle was used to hearing nothing but negative talk about Jesus. All that to say, that he was showing great belief in who Christ was saying that He was! The ***NIV Study Bible*** adds *"unless you see signs and wonders you will never believe." Was the general attitude of Galileans, not that of the official."* **4**

Devotion written by Pastor Frank & Samuel Gervasi

---

1.   Webster's Dictionary, Merriam-Webster, Inc, 2016
2.   New International Version (NIV), Holy Bible, New International Version®, NIV® Copyright ©1973, 1978, 1984, 2011 by Biblica, Inc.® Used by permission. All rights reserved worldwide.
3.   Jungle Pilot, Russel Hilt, Discovery House Publishers, 1997
4.   NIV Study Bible, BibleGatewayPlus, Biblegateway.com, as accessed on 03/20/2025

Going Deeper – A 30-Day Devotional

#4 - Praying Like a Disciple
Read: *Luke 11:1-4*

_____

"One day Jesus was praying in a certain place. When he finished, one of his disciples said to him, 'Lord, teach us to pray, just as John taught his disciples.'"
Luke 11:1, NIV

_____

Our prayer life is probably one of the most important things that we can do! That true because it's one of the most *basic* disciplines for the Christian, and every follower needs to do it. But prayer can be one that is also a misunderstood and *undertaught* topic in some churches. Additionally, it doesn't matter how long you've been a Christian because no one seems to graduate from the necessity of prayer. Christ himself realized the importance of it and prayed often. You see prayer is the thing that makes our faith real. It takes us from just mere head knowledge to living out the Christian faith. Some people pray often - and for long periods of time, but for others, it's small, short, one-line prayers - as they're going about their day. However, both types of people understand the importance of praying on a regular basis.

_____

Big Idea: *Prayer is Critical and Should Be Inspiring When Pray Like a True Disciple*

_____

The passage we are studying today is between an encounter between Jesus and His disciples regarding prayer. They had all been influenced and experienced Jesus praying daily and in various ways and with various requests. (v. 1.) So, after finishing one day his disciples ask to be taught about prayer. (v.1.) They had also experienced John the Baptist pray, as well as teach his own followers. There must have been something compelling about seeing Jesus pray or they probably wouldn't have asked. If you think about it: They grew up going to the synagogue,

Going Deeper – A 30-Day Devotional

so they had seen people pray often. Meaning, it wasn't foreign to them. In fact, they had probably been used to lengthy and lofty sounding prayers!

———————

Insight: **Consider having a prayer life that others want to emulate. It is probably one of the most encouraging things that shows our prayer life, when done correctly, can inspire others and be contagious.**

———————

One of the most popular prayers in scripture is what's known as the Lord's Prayer. Which is exactly what Christ chose to teach His disciples when asked to be taught as John the Baptist's disciples were taught. (v. 2.) *However,* giving a model or standard for prayer as opposed to actual prayer to be verbatim. In verse 2 he says: *"Father, hallowed be your name," 1* showing that we should remember who we are coming before when we pray. *"Thy kingdom come,"* implying that we should be longing for God's kingdom to be realized here on Earth during our lifetime. And prayer should also be for daily provision in life, (v.3,) when he says, *"Give us this day our daily bread."* As well as forgiveness when we fail, or others fail us. In v. 4 it says: *"Forgive us our sins, for we also forgive everyone who sins against us." 1* As well as praying for strength against life's temptation (v. 4.)

I was taught the same prayer at a young age. I always knew the words, but something seemed to be missing in the reciting of the Lord's Prayer. The actual pattern that was behind it seemed to be replaced with repetition of the words only.

John Bradford the English Reformer, prebendary of St. Paul's, and martyr said that, when he was in prayer, he never liked to rise from his knees till he began to feel something of brokenness of heart. *"Get up to your chamber, then,........if you would have a broken and contrite spirit and come not out until you have it." 2*

———————

Challenge: **What is my prayer life like currently? Do I spend regular time before God's throne, or not? How can I continue to grow in prayer?**

Pray: **Asking God to stretch my prayer life, so that I can experience Him in a fresh way....**

———————

Going Deeper:

Going Deeper – A 30-Day Devotional

The Greek term father as used in the New Testament is an understood one to the audience that Luke was reaching initially. However, the term Abba was probably more well known. Abba was Aramaic in origin and said to be a term of endearment and closeness. So, for Jesus to use it, may have been saying that we can come freely and abandon ourselves before God the Father when we bring our requests. Even the **Zondervan Illustrated Bible Backgrounds Commentary of the New Testament** addresses that: *"While it has been commonly said that Abba is a children's term meaning "daddy," this is not quite right, since Jewish adults also addressed their parents in this way. Abba was, however, a term of considerable intimacy. While Jews would sometimes refer to God as "our heavenly Father," they rarely if ever addressed him as "my father" or "father" (Abba). Jesus calls his followers to a new intimacy with God through his unique relationship with the Father."* **3**

Devotion written by Pastor Frank & Samuel Gervasi

---

1. New International Version (NIV), Holy Bible, ® Copyright ©1973, 1978, 1984, 2011 by Biblica, Inc.® Used by permission. All rights reserved worldwide.
2. Sermon Central Contributor, www.sermoncentral.com, as accessed on 03/20/2025
3. Zondervan Illustrated Bible Backgrounds Commentary of the New Testament, Copyright © 2002

Going Deeper – A 30-Day Devotional

#5 - Trust and Obey
Read: *Genesis 22:1-18*

"So, Abraham called that place The Lord Will Provide. And to this day it is said, 'On the mountain of the Lord it will be provided.'" **Genesis 22:14, NIV**

Sometimes, obedience is costly and defies logic. During the Prussian siege of Paris in the late 1800s, there was a gunner in one of the French forts named Pierre Barlot. One day, Pierre was standing by his gun when General Noel, his commander, said to him, *"Gunner, do you see the Sevres bridge over there?"* *"Yes, sir."* *"And that little shanty in a thicket of shrubs to the left of the bridge?"* *"I see it, sir,"* said Pierre. *"It's full of Prussians, I believe; try it with a shell."* Pierre turned ghostly pale. He sighted his cannon carefully, then fired it, and blew the hut to shreds. The commander Noel praised Pierre for his marksmanship but was surprised to see a single tear running down the gunner's cheek. *"What's the matter, man?"* *"Pardon me, General,"* said Pierre, *"it was my house—everything I had in the world."* **1**

Big Idea: *Faith in God, proven by deliberate and complete obedience, will always be compensated in due time.*

God commanded Abraham to show a similarly great depth of faith in what some have called Abraham's "final exam". There was no softening of the blow when God spoke to Abraham clearly in verses 2-3: *"'Take your son, your only son, whom you love – Isaac – and...sacrifice him there as a burnt offering.'"*

Don't forget how everything that God had promised Abraham about his descendants was going to be fulfilled through Isaac. Isaac was himself a miracle,

Going Deeper – A 30-Day Devotional

considering the age at which Abraham and his wife Sarah gave birth to him. Then God is asking Abraham to sacrifice the child who was the very fulfillment of His promise years earlier.

This does not sound, in our day and age, like good fatherly advice. In fact, you might receive a visit from Family Services for child-rearing like this! And yet, Abraham responds with deliberate, decisive, and complete obedience. Notice that Abraham rose "early the next morning" (v. 3). Abraham did not hesitantly delay doing what God said, he was quick and decisive to trust and obey from the moment God told him to sacrifice Isaac, his own son!

Insight: *Faith and obedience are inseparable: one cannot claim to take God at His word if he or she is not willing to do what God has said. When we say that we have faith in God, we must obey His commands.*

Additionally, Abraham is tested for his faith in this passage. He believes God at His Word and trusts Him fully, and, in response, God rewards Abraham for his faith. First, God provides a way out of the demanding situation by providing a ram in a thicket *"caught by its horns"* (v. 13) to be sacrificed in Isaac's place. At the very last moment, when Abraham is about to go through with the unimaginable, God provides a way out.

Then finally, God Himself rewards Abraham's faithfulness by renewing the covenant in verses16-18: *"'I swear by myself, declares the LORD, that because you have done this and not.*
withheld your son, your only son, I will surely bless you and make your descendants as numerous as the stars in the sky...and through your offspring all nations on earth will be blessed, because you have obeyed me.'"

God may never ask us to trust Him for something so great. But He does ask all of us, at various times, to trust Him for something. And complete faith, proven by obedience, will always be compensated in due time.

Challenge: *What is God asking me to have faith with? How can I grow in trusting and*
obeying God?

Going Deeper – A 30-Day Devotional

Pray: *Asking God to help me trust Him no matter the circumstances and obey fully no matter how difficult.*

Going Deeper:

In Hebrews 11, the Hall of Faith, Abraham is one of those commended for his faith in verses 17-19: *"By faith Abraham, when he was tested, offered up Isaac; and he who received the promises was offering up his only begotten son; it was he to whom it was said, 'In Isaac your seed shall be called.' He that considered that God is able to raise men even from the dead."*

The **NIV Study Bible** says regarding these verses:
"If you are afraid to trust God with your most prized possession, dream, or person, pay attention to Abraham's example. Because Abraham was willing to give up everything for God, he received back more than he could have imagined."
2

Devotion written by Pastor Frank & Samuel Gervasi

---

1. Ministry127, https://ministry127.com/resources/illustration/the-cost-of-obedience, as accessed on 08/25/2024.
2. Zondervan NIV Life Application Study Bible. Ronald A Beers, gen. ed. Zondervan. Copyright 2011

Going Deeper – A 30-Day Devotional

#6 - Forgiveness is Not Optional
Read: *Matthew 18:21-35*

_____

"Then Peter came to Jesus and asked, 'Lord, how many times shall I forgive my brother or sister who sins against me? Up to seven times?'" **Matthew 18:21, NIV**

_____

Just before Easter in 2009, Fred Winters, pastor of the First Baptist Church in Maryville, Illinois, was shot and killed during a Sunday morning service by a disturbed young man. The tragedy shocked the church and the pastor's family, but it did not destroy their faith. The next week the newly widowed Cindy Winters was interviewed on a national news broadcast. When asked about her husband's killer she said, *"I do not have any hatred or even hard feelings toward him. We have been praying for him." 1* We may never have to forgive someone for something so tragic, but we are **_ALL_** called to forgive at one time or another.

_____

Big Idea: *Forgiveness is not optional and costly and will require something of us to pardon others when they have hurt us.*

_____

In today's bible passage we see a parable where Peter asks Jesus an important question regarding forgiveness. *"Then Peter came to Jesus and asked, 'Lord, how many times shall I forgive my brother or sister who sins against me? Up to seven times?'"* (v. 21.) Even though it sounds like a straightforward question it may have been rooted in what was taught during those times. The main teaching regarding the topic by Jewish leaders of that day was traditionally up to three times a person should be forgiven to fulfill Mosaic Law.

Going Deeper – A 30-Day Devotional

So, for Peter to ask up to seven times it may have been a way to seem *ultra-spiritual* before his mentor. However, Jesus raises the bar for His followers by giving such a large number. In verse 22 it says that *"Jesus answered, 'I tell you, not seven times, but seventy-seven times.'"* Which was an even bigger number than what many were used to hearing. Implying that God doesn't want us to keep track of how often we forgive others.

Additionally, another aspect regarding forgiveness is that it usually will cost us something when a person makes the choice to forgive an offense. Whether that is just the financial cost of a real debt, or an emotional debt from being hurt.

In the parable Jesus tells of a king that wanted to settle an account of a servant that owed him about twenty years of a day-laborer's wages and could not pay, (verses 23-24.) Nevertheless, when the servant could not pay the debt and he begged the king to forgive the debt, he was released. (v. 25.)

———

Insight: *Forgiveness will cost a person something and we should reciprocate to others like our heavenly Father forgives us – avoiding hypocrisy...*

———

When the servant was put in a similar situation, for an even smaller amount, he did not forgive the person that was indebted to him. Then, went and had him thrown into prison until the debt could be paid, verses 28-30. *"But when that servant went out, he found one of his fellow servants who owed him a hundred silver coins...... 'Pay back what you owe me!' he demanded. "But he refused. Instead, he went off and had the man thrown into prison until he could pay the debt'"* (v. 28, 30.) Jesus paid the price for our forgiveness with the high price of death on a Cross. We should also reciprocate and forgive others! There is a saying I once saw, and it says: *"What sets Christians apart from the world is the obligation and compulsion to forgive." (Unknown)*

———

Challenge: *Who do I need to forgive for an offense? Am I keeping count of when someone wrongs me?*

Pray: *Asking God to help us forgive no matter the circumstances and no matter how many times we have been hurt.*

———

Going Deeper:

Going Deeper – A 30-Day Devotional

In the *Talmud* which was the central rabbinic teaching for Judaism instructed that people were to forgive up to three times. However, after that there was no longer an obligation to forgive another individual. At least in what was required when obeying Mosaic Law.

The **NIV Grace and Truth Study Bible** says, *"Within Judaism, forgiving someone three times was enough to show a forgiving spirit (Job 33:29–30; Am 1:3.) Peter's suggestion seven times shows generosity. Jesus' response is not about a specific number but is an instruction to forgive without keeping count. He illustrates this with a parable in which a servant owes his king an incalculable debt, at least 2.5 billion dollars in today's terms. The point is the immensity of the debt and the impossibility of paying it back. The king orders that the servant and all he has be sold into debtor's slavery, a common practice in the ancient world that was designed both as a punishment and as a means to repayment (cf. 2Ki 4:1; Ne 5:4–8)."* **2** Additionally, some versions of the Bible say seventy-seven times which is a large number, even much more generous than the seven times Peter suggested. However, some manuscripts suggest that it was seventy times seven which is four hundred and ninety times.

———————————

Devotion written by Pastor Frank & Samuel Gervasi

———————————

1. Ministry127, https://ministry127.com/resources/illustrations/forgiveness, as accessed on 03/20/2025.
2. NIV Grace and Truth Study Bible, Copyright © 2021 by Zondervan, 2011, BibleGatewayPlus, , www.biblegateway.com, as accessed on 03/20/2025.

Going Deeper – A 30-Day Devotional

#7 - Enduring Prayer
Read: *Luke 18:1-8*

""Ask and it will be given to you; seek and you will find; knock and the door will be opened to you."' **Matthew 7:7, NIV**

A fisherman was at sea with his godless companions when a storm came up and threatened to sink their ship. His friends begged him to pray; but he said, *"It's been a long time since I've done that or even entered a church."* At their insistence, however, he finally cried out, *"O Lord, I haven't asked anything of You in 15 years, and if You help us now and bring us safely to land, I promise I won't bother You again for another 15!"* Unfortunately, many people view prayer as an escape mechanism rather than a constant line of communication with God. *1* Prayer is necessary for our relationship with God. However, when the answer is long in coming, we should continue to pray.

Big Idea: *We should be persistent in prayer and never give up even when the request is taking long in being answered*

The passage we're looking at is from the Gospel of Luke. And in it, Jesus was teaching about prayer and how we should persevere over time when we need to. So, he does it by telling a parable to make his point, involving an unjust judge and a widow. So, there are many variables that come into play as well.

First, Jesus was teaching a parable to His disciples. However, obviously speaking to all people who call themselves Christ followers and would read this. Additionally, we also know that parables are stories used to teach spiritual truth. So maybe they happened, maybe not but it doesn't really matter anyway when it comes to applying them to our lives.

Going Deeper – A 30-Day Devotional

We saw that the story contained some main characters, like a judge, a widow, and an unnamed adversary. (vv. 1-3.) We read in v. 2 *"That there was a certain judge who neither feared God ----nor cared about men."* Which I think says a lot about this judge's mindset because he really didn't seem to care about what this widow even needed. Much different than our God because He is one cares *intimately* about all that concerns us always.

However, something that I think stands out is the widow's request. Because Luke records the term *"adversary."* Verse 3 says: *"And there was a widow in that town who kept coming to him with the plea, 'Grant me justice against my adversary.'"* One version uses the word *"opponent"* and this is an interesting word because it actually carries this idea of an opponent much like in a law suit. Which explains why she was going to a judge in the first place: to seek justice from the unjust judge. (v.2) Nevertheless, the Judge was not fair or even concerned about people in general. *So why would this judge help the window?* Regardless of the details he did grant her request because of her persistence and tenacity. (vv. 4-5) *"'Even though I do not fear God nor respect man, 5 yet because this widow bothers me, I will give her legal protection, otherwise by continually coming she will wear me out.'"* So, *if* the unjust judge will grant justice, how much more will God hear the prayers of His children? God longs to give the best for His children, so we should come freely and with abandon before His throne.

––––––––

Insight: *We should pray with determination and perseverance because it keeps us focused on the need, especially when the answer is long.*

––––––––

Now we may not be in case of needing a judge to decide a case for us, but we all have needs. Regardless of what it is, endurance is usually needed and would be wise in being persistent in prayer. There is a saying I once heard and it goes like this: *"We should pray, then pray more, and after that pray even more."* *(Unknown)*

––––––––

Challenge: *Am I persistent in prayer? Or do I give up easily when it comes to prayer?*

Pray: **Asking God to give us the endurance we need to pray over the long haul when needed.**

––––––––

Going Deeper:

Going Deeper – A 30-Day Devotional

Consider the widow in the parable because they were said to be very needy in that time and culture. Much different than today because widows are very independent and do many things for themselves. In fact, we have widows today and they take care of themselves and are independent in many cases. However, in that day widows were very dependent on others just like in the parable. One source says: *"The widow was a helpless person with nothing but right on her side. She wanted justice, not revenge."* (ESV Reformation Study Bible, Ligonier, 2015) Additionally, **The Expositor's Bible Commentary** says, *"The theme is that of the vindication of God's misunderstood and suffering people. God's people in OT days needed to "wait" on God as he worked out justice with apparent slowness (see Ps 25:2-3). In the final days the martyrs wait for vindication (Rev 6:9-11). Meanwhile we wrestle with the problem of evil and with issues of theodicy. Under these circumstances we should "always pray and not give up."* **2**

———————

Devotion written by Pastor Frank & Samuel Gervasi

———————

1. Ministry127, https://ministry127.com/resources/illustrations/prayer, as accessed on 03/20/2025
2. Expositor's Bible Commentary (Abridged Edition): New Testament Copyright 2004., Bible Gateway Plus, www.biblegateway.com, as accessed on 03/20/2025

Going Deeper – A 30-Day Devotional

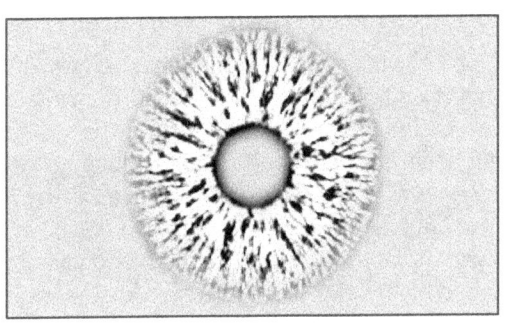

#8 – Eye in The Sky
Read: *Psalm 121*

"The LORD will watch over your coming and going both now and forevermore."
Psalm 121:8, NIV

King salmon, also known as Chinook salmon, lead an incredible life. After spending most of their lives in the ocean, Chinook salmon embark on a migration back to the same freshwater streams where they were born to lay their own eggs. This journey often covers several thousand miles and requires the salmon to swim against the strong force of the current. Yet every year, thousands can be seen swimming in a caravan to go back to the place where they were born.

The Israelites often made a similarly difficult journey, albeit a shorter distance. Every year, the Israelites would come up from all their towns and villages to the temple in Jerusalem for the annual feasts. The road was often long and difficult, and there were dangers of inclement weather, wild animals, and bandits along the way. During this journey, it was customary for the travelers to sing a "song of ascent" – one of 14 psalms specially designed for these travelers, including our psalm today.

Big Idea: *God's watchful care is reliable, tailor-made, and motivated by love.*

The psalmist's dependence on God during this journey is clear in verses 1-2: *"I lift my eyes up to the mountain – where does my help come from? My help comes from the LORD, the Maker of heaven and earth."* Notice that the Psalmist doesn't

Going Deeper – A 30-Day Devotional

depend on his own knowledge as his source of strength; he doesn't turn to money or place his trust in a government official. The writer is confident and convinced that his help comes from the Living God, the, *"...Maker of heaven and earth."* We see three reasons for his confidence. For one, the Psalmist knows that God's assistance is reliable, as we see in verse 3: *"He will not let your foot slip; he who watches you will not slumber..."* This is a great image, when you think about it, because people get tired and run down, and our bodies are made to need rest. But God is not limited by the same restrictions. He never grows tired or weary (Isaiah 40:28-31); His care is reliable and never lacking!

Insight: **When God is watching over a person, He will provide exactly what is needed in life, because nothing is hidden from His sight. He knows every detail of our lives; therefore, we can trust His watchful care.**

The Psalmist also recognizes that God's care is tailor-made. In verse 5, the Psalmist makes the distinction that, *"The LORD watches over you..."* Implying that God's care is specific to us and our lives.

Then finally, the writer trusts God's care because it is motivated by love. Look again at v. 8: *"The LORD will watch over your coming and going both now and forevermore."* I heard it said like this before: "God's care for us is more watchful and more tender than any human father could possibly be...and **nothing** can change His love for you!" God's love never weakens or fades and will watch over us forever. Many people turn to many different things for strength and comfort in life. Some are valid and make sense, and some don't. But we, as children of God, have the best place to turn when life gets hard or we find ourselves in a confusing situation. The God of the universe intimately cares for and has His eye on us.

Challenge: **Where do I turn when I need assistance? How can I learn to trust God's care in my life?**

Pray: **Asking God to help me trust the help He provides and not rely on my own understanding or strength....**

Going Deeper:

Going Deeper – A 30-Day Devotional

Many believe that this psalm was written by King Hezekiah, the 13th ruler of the southern kingdom of Judah in the Old Testament. Throughout his reign, Hezekiah was responsible for nationwide spiritual reform, because they had become a people who had grown apathetic toward the things of God. Hezekiah's leadership sparked national revival, as the people reopened the doors to the Temple and put aside their idols. Hezekiah was said to have a close relationship with God, which I think is evident because you can tell that he relied fully on God for help – just like we should!

The *Bible Knowledge Commentary* says this about songs of ascent: *"The title 'song of ascent' identifies each of Psalms 120-134 as a pilgrim song to be sung when the Israelites 'ascended' (went up) to Jerusalem for the annual feasts. Four of these 15 psalms are ascribed to David (Ps. 122; 124; 131; 133), 1 to Solomon (Ps. 127), and the other 10 are anonymous. ...The pilgrim-psalmist [in Psalm 121], as he contemplated his journey through the hills to Jerusalem, asked where his help came from. He found the answer to his question in the affirmation of his faith that the LORD, who created heaven and earth – with those hills – was his only Source of help."* **1**

Devotion written by Pastor Frank & Samuel Gervasi

---

1. Walvoord, John F. and Roy B. Zuck, Psalm 120,-A. Contemplation of the Journey, The Bible Knowledge Commentary, SP Publications, Inc., 1985, pg. 882-883.

Going Deeper – A 30-Day Devotional

#9 – "Grace in Action"
Read: *John 8:1-11*

———————

"When they persisted in asking him, he straightened up and said to them, 'He who is without sin among you, let him be the first to throw a stone at her.'" **John 8:7, NIV**

———————

I heard a story once about a pastor who, one Sunday morning, found the roads to his church blocked. Due to this unexpected obstacle, he was forced to skate on the river to get there. When he arrived, the elders of the church were horrified to learn that their preacher had skated on Sunday – the Lord's Day!. After the service they held a meeting where the pastor explained that it was either skate to church or not go at all. After a pause, one elder asked, "Did you enjoy it?" When the preacher answered, "No," the board cleared him of wrongdoing. *1*

In our passage today, we find a similarly legalistic group of Pharisees bringing before Jesus a woman caught in adultery. From verse 6, we learn that, *"They were using this question to trap him...",* and make Him say something that would discredit His reputation. Instead, Christ responded with wisdom, and modeled to us the mindset we should have when it comes to grace.

———————

Big Idea: *Grace looks beyond the letter of the law to a person's heart, bringing forgiveness, restoration, conviction, and change.*

———————

The adulterous woman's accusers were *"the teachers of the law and the Pharisees"* (v. 2), both of which went to great lengths to follow Mosaic Law. In

Going Deeper – A 30-Day Devotional

fact, these religious leaders were correct in what Mosaic Law prescribed regarding the punishment for adultery (v. 5). However, they completely threw mercy and compassion out the window in the process, and their real intentions behind this episode were dishonest and self-serving.

But whereas the religious leaders condemned the woman for her failure, Jesus responds with grace: *"When they persisted in asking him, he straightened up and said to them, 'He who is without sin among you, let him be the first to throw a stone at her.'"* (v. 7)

He didn't have to do a lot, did He? Jesus' question itself brought conviction to the religious leaders and caused them to evaluate their own lives. And in response, *"...they began leaving one by one..."* (v. 9), for none present could claim that they had never sinned.

––––––––––––––

Insight: **Grace not only pardons and forgives us but causes us to pursue holy living. When we understand the power of grace, we don't want to abuse it in any way. Grace should always produce change and lead us to something better.**

––––––––––––––

In the end, only Jesus and the woman remained. Notice how he didn't yell at her or attack her. He didn't ask, "What's wrong with you? I can't believe you fell again!" Instead, *"...Jesus said, 'I do not condemn you either. Go. From now on, do not sin any longer.'"* (v. 11) Some versions translate it as, *"'Then neither do I condemn you. Go now and **leave your life of sin**.'"* It was the grace that was shown that day that probably changed that woman forever!

The same is true for us. It is ultimately the grace that God has shown to us that acquits us of our wrongdoings, forgives us, empowers us, and prompts us to change. And because it was freely shown to us, we should show it to others as well! I heard one person say it like this: *"The people who tend to be the most gracious are those who know how badly they need grace."* Unknown

––––––––––––––

Challenge: **How might I see the power of grace that causes change in my own life? How can I grow in grace?**

Going Deeper – A 30-Day Devotional

Pray: __Pray:__   _Thanking God for the grace He's shown to me and praying for help to show that grace to others...._

Going Deeper:

Warren Wiersbe once said this:

"We must not misinterpret this event to mean that Jesus was easy on sin or that He contradicted the law. For Jesus to forgive this woman meant that He had to one day die for her sins. Forgiveness is free, but it is not cheap. Furthermore, Jesus perfectly fulfilled the law so that no one could justly accuse Him of opposing its teachings or weakening its power...

The law was given to reveal sin (Rom. 3:20), and we must be condemned by the law before we can be cleansed by God's grace. Law and grace do not compete; they complement each other. Nobody was ever saved by keeping the law, but nobody was ever saved by grace who was not first indicted by the law. There must be conviction before there can be conversion." **2**

Devotion written by Pastor Frank & Samuel Gervasi

---

1.   Today in the Word, Moody Publishers, December 1989, p. 12
2.   Warren Wiersbe, Copyright © Warren W. Wiersbe.

Going Deeper – A 30-Day Devotional

#10 - Learning to Speak Wisely?
Read: *James 3:1-12*

"For if we could control our tongues, we would be perfect and could also control ourselves in every other way." **James 3:2b, NIV**

A husband and wife tell a story about how recently they *"sat down to eat in a local restaurant."* And the husband, *"had gone to the restroom and when the server came over to get our drink orders, my wife said, 'We'll both have water, and I'll have iced tea. I don't know what he'll drink.' The server responded, 'So what's he going to do with the water?'"* **1**

Our words are powerful and can be used in a positive but also negative way causing harm if not careful. In our passage today, in the book of James. It's one where he compares our speech with three different things, a fire, a ship, and a horse. And each one has something in common, a small thing having a big effect.

Big Idea: *Our Speech is Powerful! –So, We Should Use Caution When We Speak.*

Even though our tongues are a small part of our bodies, our words can have big effects, can't they? And we can use them for good or we can allow them to destroy and hurt other people. We saw in verse 5: *"Even so the tongue is a little member and boasts great things."*

Going Deeper – A 30-Day Devotional

Even though James uses the word tongue he's obviously referring to our speech, the words we say and the things that come out of our mouths. What comes out of our mouths when we interact with those around us, ---matters to God.

James describes our tongue as something small but powerful in verse 5b-6: "A small thing that makes grand speeches. But a tiny spark can set a great forest on fire." I think it's an excellent picture when he's talking about our speech. Because some of the World's largest and most destructive forest fires all started with one spark.

Insight: Even Though it's Difficult Our Speech Should Be Mastered - So We Can Live Wisely!

Nevertheless, even though it's difficult we can't use it as an excuse because God still wants us to use our speech in a way that honors Him. So, we need to learn to discipline our speech, regardless of the difficulty.

If we look starting in v. 7, James likens our speech with all the various animals that have been tamed by man. However, our speech being very difficult to master. "For every species of beasts and birds, of reptiles and creatures of the sea, is tamed and has been tamed by the human race. But no one can tame the tongue; it is a restless evil and full of deadly poison."

God cares about how we use our speech, and our words should be controlled because they are powerful. So, we should learn to use our speech in ways that build others up and encourage them. I heard one person say: "you can tell a person's character by the words he or she uses!" (unknown)

Challenge: *How might I use my speech to build others up and not tear down? How can I speak in an edifying way?*

Pray: *Thanking God for the ability to use my speech in a good way. Asking for the power I need to master it....*

Going Deeper:

Going Deeper – A 30-Day Devotional

The term here *"perfect"* in verse 2 is not referring to absence of fault. However, it is speaking of the *"spiritual maturity"* that Christians should be striving for. The **NIV Study Bible Notes** also confirms and expands on this important word by saying that if a person could tame their tongue, it would most likely filter over into other areas of their life as well.

"Since the tongue is so difficult to control, those who control it perfectly gain control of themselves in all other areas of life as well. James indicates that complete control of the tongue, if it were possible, would render a person 'perfect.' This reflects the same Greek term from 1:4, where it indicates 'maturity.'"

Even though it is difficult, we should learn to master our speech in a way that helps and *not* hurts others. **Ephesians 4:29** is the standard that was set by the apostle Paul as well when he says: *"Let no [a]unwholesome word proceed from your mouth, but only such a word as is good for edification [b]according to the need of the moment, so that it will give grace to those who hear." 2*

—————————————

Devotion written by Pastor Frank & Samuel Gervasi

—————————————

1. Speaker Stories, https://speakerstories.wordpress.com/2012/04/16/people-are-funny/, as accessed on 03/20/2025.
2. NIV Study Bible, Copyright © 1985, 1995, 2002, 2008, 2011 by Zondervan.

Going Deeper – A 30-Day Devotional

Going Deeper – A 30-Day Devotional

#11 Confidence in God
Read: *Psalm 146:3-6*

"But joyful are those who have the God of Israel as their helper, whose hope is in the Lord their God." *Psalm 146:5, NIV*

There is a story about a father who went rock climbing with his son, Zac. The two were out in the country, climbing around in some cliffs, when the father heard a voice from above him yell, "Hey Dad! Catch me!" He turned around to see Zac joyfully jumping off a rock straight toward him. He had jumped first and then yelled "Hey Dad!" Things became an instant circus act, as the father moved into position to catch him. Both fell to the ground. When the father found his voice again, he gasped in exasperation: "Zac! Can you give me one good reason why you did that???" He responded with remarkable calmness: "Sure...because you're my dad." *1*

We all place our trust in someone or something. Many times, we choose to trust other people, expecting them to be looking out for us. In some situations, that trust is well-placed, like with Zac and his dad. But other times we place our confidence in the wrong people for the wrong things. As we'll see in our devotion today, there is only one Person in whom we should be placing our ultimate confidence. And we should be overflowing with thankfulness when we realize just how reliable He is.

Big Idea: We should never place our confidence in people but rather give our trust and worship to God.

Going Deeper – A 30-Day Devotional

Last week, we saw how Psalm 146 exhorts us to worship joyfully before God, and in these verses, we now see one of the reasons we should give God that praise: people fail, but God does not. Look at vv. 3-4: *"Don't put your confidence in powerful people; there is no help for you there. When they breathe their last, they return to the earth, and all their plans die with them."*

We can see something clearly in these verses: God may be worthy of our adoration, but people will never measure up in the same ways. And that will be true of even the best, wisest, most respectable person we could know. They will still always be lacking, because they will always be limited to what extent they can help us.

Insight: Trust and praise have a symbiotic relationship. When we choose to place our confidence in God, we are moved to worship Him. Likewise, when we worship God even in the harshest trials, we find it easier to have faith in God's perfect plan.

Verse 3 describes *"powerful people"* or some versions say *"princes"*. We can all picture someone who fits this description – someone with influence and status. Nevertheless, even these people will let us down at one point or another.

But isn't it good news to know that God will never let us down? Look at the contrast between vv. 3-4 (which we read earlier) and vv. 5-6: *"But joyful are those who have the God of Israel as their helper, whose hope is in the LORD their God. He made heaven and earth, the sea, and everything in them. He keeps every promise forever."*

Even the most trustworthy people on earth will fall short and fail us, but we serve the never-failing God of Armies. How should we respond? The psalmist responds in jubilant praise! Throughout the rest of the psalm, he demonstrates his thankfulness and gratitude for the faithfulness and reliability of his King. Let's offer our trust and affection to God as well and choose to place our confidence in Him rather than fallible human beings. And let's worship joyfully before the Lord!

Going Deeper – A 30-Day Devotional

Challenge: Where have I been placing my confidence? What do I need to trust God with today?

Pray: Asking God to help me place my confidence in His unfailing nature and not in mere mortals, and thanking Him for unsurpassed faithfulness

Going Deeper:

Matthew Henry, in his Commentary on the Whole Bible, says regarding verses 3-4: "*David is supposed to have penned this psalm; and he was himself a prince, a mighty prince; as such, it might be thought...that he himself, having been so great a blessing to his country, should be adored, according to the usage of the heathen nations, who deified their heroes, that they should all come and trust in his shadow and make him their stay and strong-hold. 'No,' says David, 'Put not your trust in princes (Ps. 146:3), not in me, not in any other; do not repose your confidence in them; do not raise your expectations from them. Be not too sure of their sincerity; some thought they knew better how to reign by knowing how to dissemble. Be not too sure of their constancy and fidelity; it is possible they may both change their minds and break their words.' But though we suppose them very wise and as good as David himself, yet we must not be too sure of their ability and continuance, for they are sons of Adam, weak and mortal. There is indeed a Son of man in whom there is help, in whom there is salvation, and who will not fail those that trust in him.*" **2**

Devotion written by Pastor Frank & Samuel Gervasi

---

1. Adapted from https://www.sermonillustrations.com/a-z/t/trust.htm; as accessed on 11/20/2024
2. Matthew Henry's Commentary on the Whole Bible, public domain.

Going Deeper – A 30-Day Devotional

Going Deeper – A 30-Day Devotional

#12 - God's Useful Book
Read: *2 Timothy 3:14-17*

"All Scripture is God-breathed and is useful for teaching, rebuking, correcting and training in righteousness, 17 so that the servant of God may be thoroughly equipped for every good work." **2 Timothy 3:16-17, NIV**

"A Roman Catholic priest in Belgium rebuked a young woman and her brother for reading that 'bad book' pointing to the Bible. 'Mr. Priest,' she replied, 'a little while ago my brother was an idler, a gambler, a drunkard, and made such a noise in the house that no one could stay in it. Since he began to read the Bible, he works with industry, goes no longer to the tavern, no longer touches cards, brings home money to his poor old mother, and our life at home is quiet and delightful. How comes it, Mr. Priest, that a bad book produces such good fruits?'" **1**

The Bible is transformative and can change people for the good. In fact, it has been said by some to be a divinely fortified book-not just any book- so it can be believed fully. That is probably true for several reasons however, because it's not just some great literary work, like we might see in a university, or a library, or even in a bookstore. We can place our trust in its reliability because it's more of a literary miracle, if anything. There really can't be anything earthly compared with it, because it's not earthly in its origin.

Consider, that a group of individuals didn't sit on a committee and even plan the sixty-six books of the Bible. Rather, more than forty different authors labored for over a span of sixty generations and over three continents. We saw in v. 16 that:

Going Deeper – A 30-Day Devotional

"All Scripture is God-breathed." Carrying this idea that it came directly from God's mouth and speaking through everyday people of various backgrounds.

_____

Big Idea: *The Bible Came from God's mouth, through the individual writers-affirming its useability....*

_____

The Bible is also an especially *pertinent* book with uses that lead to spiritual growth because it's not a book that is just useful for something trivial, or something just to pass the time. It's a book that has a clear, decisive and important function, that's relevant for all things. However, it's especially useful for the matter in the spiritual growth of anyone.

In v.16 it says: *"All Scripture, is God-breathed and is useful for teaching, rebuking, correcting and training in righteousness."*

He lists clear benefits or uses that come from God's word that even though he was telling Timothy about, are for really everyone, regardless of who we are. One version uses the word *"profitable"* which I kind of like, because it's kind of just gets your attention more than *useful*. That we can profit when we read the bible is encouraging to say the least. He also expands in v. 16 when he says: *"Teaching, rebuking, correcting."* All things that are needed at different seasons of a Christ follower's life in many cases.

_____

Insight: *The Bible is Useful for Training in Righteousness -That We May Be Equipped!*

_____

Finally, we don't read the Bible not to acquire information or be puffed up with knowledge but that we grow in faith, holiness, and purity. In the last part of v. 16 the Apostle Paul was giving Timothy the final goal of the Bible, *"and training in righteousness."* God's ultimate desire for his children is that we all grow in righteousness and apply what we learn. There is probably no book that's more relevant for today's culture, even though it may look different than the culture of the day.

_____

Going Deeper – A 30-Day Devotional

Challenge: *When might I spend more time reading God's Word? How can I grow in holiness applying the bible in greater ways?*

Pray: *Asking God for the desire and wisdom to learn the Scriptures in a greater way and apply them....*

Going Deeper:

Context might clarify the times that were prevalent during the writing of first and second Timothy. There were a lot of different works that were popular, however, written works were not as readily available as today. However, both Jews and Christians were relying heavily on Old Testament Scrolls and the new letters and epistles that were being circulated among the churches. In fact, *Zondervan Illustrated Bible Backgrounds Commentary of the New Testament* says:

"The religions of Greece and Rome in Paul's time were not dependent on written materials. There were sacred books containing oracular materials (e.g., the Sibylline Oracles), magic books with spells, incantations, charms, and so forth (cf. Acts 19:19), and other kinds of handbooks on practices such as augury (the interpretation of various omens). Moreover, the writing of the ancient poets like Homer or Hesiod were regarded as having particular authority in their myths about the gods, though at the same time there was a popular saying: 'The poets tell many lies,' especially about the gods. In contrast, both Judaism and its offspring, Christianity, were and are religions that rely heavily on the inspired and authoritative Scriptures." 2

Devotion written by Pastor Frank & Samuel Gervasi

---

1. Ministry 127, https://ministry127.com/resources/illustration/the-fruit-of-the-bible/ as accessed on 09/15/2024
2. (Zondervan Illustrated Bible Backgrounds Commentary of the New Testament, Copyright © 2002. All rights reserved.

Going Deeper – A 30-Day Devotional

#13 – Follow Me
Read: *Luke 14:25-35*

_____

"And whoever does not carry their cross and follow me cannot be my disciple."
Luke 14:27, NIV

_____

Phillip "Jim" Eliot was an evangelist and Christian missionary who died pursuing his life's ambition of taking the gospel to unreached people. On January 8, 1956, he and four American missionary companions were speared to death on a remote beach by ten men of the primitive Auca/Waorani tribe—the tribe he had felt called to evangelize.

Yet Jim Eliot's widow, Elisabeth, held no grudges toward her husband's murderers. Instead, she and several other women moved to the Auca village to continue the work their husbands began. Just one year after the five missionaries were slain in Ecuador, she wrote, *"We have proved beyond any doubt that [God] means what He says – His grace is sufficient, nothing can separate us from the love of Christ. We pray that if any, anywhere, are fearing that the cost of discipleship is too great, that they may be given to glimpse that treasure in heaven promised to all who forsake."* **1**

_____

<u>Big Idea</u>: *Jesus wants every part of our lives, both spiritual and physical, devoted to Him and His kingdom.*

_____

Going Deeper – A 30-Day Devotional

Sometimes the Christian life can demand a lot from the believer. In a spiritual sense, following Jesus can always seem to stretch a person, because everybody brings a different background, character flaws, and ways of doing things that God wants to alter. Even physically, believers may experience sickness and disease that God uses for His glory.

In our passage today, we can clearly see that Jesus wants first place in our lives for all things. He wants our full allegiance, and the deepest place in our hearts. We see in verse 26: *"If anyone comes to me and does not hate father and mother, wife and children...even their own life – such a person **cannot** be my disciple."* (emphasis added)

To clarify, Jesus is not saying that people should despise their families; families are a gift from God (Matthew 15:4; 1 Timothy 5:8). Rather, Jesus is saying we should be so thoroughly and passionately dedicated to Him, that our love for other things pales in comparison so much, it's like hatred. To be a disciple, you must love Jesus more than those relationships.

Insight: *We must understand our commitment in walking with Christ, so we aren't discouraged when life gets hard. Because following Jesus is the most important decision a person can make. God wants whole-hearted disciples that are committed to complete surrender.*

Sometimes, that wholehearted allegiance means dying to the old ways of life. Look at verse 27: *"Whoever does not carry their cross and follow me cannot be my disciple."* Think about that – Jesus wants our goals, our plans, and our dreams submitted completely for His use. To be identified with Christ means dying to old ways, old thought patterns, even old relationships if they hinder our walk with the Lord. Finally, look at verse 33: *"In the same way, those of you who do not give up everything you have **cannot** be my disciples."* It doesn't get much clearer than that! Our families, our careers, our desires, even the tangible things we take for granted, belong to God. And when we lay those things at His feet to follow Him, we'll find it was the best place to put them.

Going Deeper – A 30-Day Devotional

Dietrich Bonhoeffer once said this: *"Salvation is free, but discipleship will cost you your life." 2*

Challenge: **What does it cost me to follow Jesus? What does it mean to be identified with Christ?**

Pray: **Praying for God to help me follow Him, no matter what it costs me**

Going Deeper:

Verse 34 says, *"Salt is good, but if it loses its saltiness, how can it be made salty again? It is fit neither for the soil nor for the manure pile; it is thrown out."* Regarding this verse, the John MacArthur Study Bible says this: *"Salt was an essential item in first-century Palestine...In a hot climate, without refrigeration, salt was the practical means of preserving food." 3*

In the same way, we should leave others that we encounter wanting to know more about our faith.

Devotion written by Pastor Frank & Samuel Gervasi

---

1.   Christianity Today, Vol. 1, reprinted Vol. 40, no. 10, https://www.gotquestions.org/Jim-Elliot.html, as accessed on 03/20/2025
2.   Dietrich Bonhoffer, The Cost of Discipleship, pg. 39, New York: Macmillan Publishing Company, 1963; first published, 1937.
3.   MacArthur Study Bible, Bible Gateway Plus, www.biblrgateway.com, Copyright © John F. MacArthur, published by Thomas Nelson, 2006.

Going Deeper – A 30-Day Devotional

#14 - Doing Your Best
Read: *Galatians 6:1-10*

_____

"Let us not become weary in doing good, for at the proper time we will reap a harvest if we do not give up." **Galatians 6:9, NIV**

_____

"It took less than ten seconds for Jamaican sprinter Usain Bolt to cover the one-hundred-meter distance on the Olympic track and win the gold medal in London. Those few seconds cemented his status as the "fastest man alive" and placed him on the winner's podium once again. But the race was not won in those seconds—it was won by hours and hours of practice, workouts, weightlifting, special diet, and coaching. The race was not won in the performance but in the preparation. It is our desire for something greater that causes us to sacrifice some things, even some good things, for the sake of things that are better." **1**

_____

Big Idea: *Doing Our Best is God's Will and Will Pay off in the Long Run.*

_____

We may not make the same sacrifices an athlete makes, but we all must lay down a natural human tendency of complacency and pride, and choose to do our best, especially in matters of our faith. The Apostle Paul admonishes us in verse 4 to *"do good to everyone"*, and to *"share each other's burdens, and in this way obey the law of Christ."* v. 2

Going Deeper – A 30-Day Devotional

These verses aren't saying that believers should follow *Mosaic* Law; rather, he was speaking in a fashion that some in that church understood. Although we are no longer under the Law, it's clear that doing good and living like Jesus *(the "law of Christ")* is pleasing to the Lord.

Doing good starts with looking at ourselves first. We see in verses 4-5: *"Pay careful attention to your **own** work, for then you will get the satisfaction of a job well done, and then you won't need to compare yourself to anyone else."* (NIV) This is good advice for all of us, because something gets lost when our attention starts focusing on what others should be doing. Although it may be difficult, we need to focus on our walk with Christ if we want to do our best, understanding that *"You are not that important."* v. 3b

_____

Insight: *We will reap what we sow in life. Although God often graciously gives us what we don't deserve, it is a natural law of God that the more a person lives to please their flesh, the more death and decay they experience. We cannot live however we want; we must choose to live according to God's Word if we want to do our best and receive our reward.*

_____

Finally, look at verses 9-10: *"So, let us not become weary in doing what is good. At just the right time we will reap a harvest of blessings if we do not give up. Therefore, whenever we have the opportunity, we should do good to everyone, especially in the family of faith."* (NIV) Doing our best will always pay off in due time. We may not see it right away. We may not see it next month, or even next year. But God has promised He will bless those who do their best, in whatever form that blessing He chooses.

Notice that these verses say, *"**we will** reap a harvest"*. This phrase sounds definitive in the fact that those who do good will be rewarded by God's own hand. But notice that that harvest only comes *"if we do not give up"*. Don't be discouraged if the waiting is getting long; giving our best to God and obeying the law of Christ will be worth it in the end. Stand strong and continue choosing to do good until your harvest comes.

_____

Challenge: *How can I do good to those around me? How can I grow in doing good?*

Pray: *Praying for God to help me persevere until the harvest comes, giving my best to Him and following His will...*

_____

Going Deeper:

Regarding the principle of reaping and sowing, the CSB *Tony Evans Study Bible* says this:

"God has established certain laws that govern the universe he has made. This is true in the physical world (e.g., the law of gravity). But it's true of the spiritual world as well. Paul articulates an important spiritual law or principle when he says, whatever a person sows he will also reap. A farmer harvests exactly what he plants. If he sows potatoes, he won't be looking to harvest green beans. Decide what you want to harvest spiritually and let that control what you decide to sow. This law is universal (it applies to all people everywhere) and inviolable (it proves true without fail). Don't kid yourself into believing that you can rebel against God without consequence." 2

_____

Devotion written by Pastor Frank & Samuel Gervasi

_____

1. Ministry 127, https://ministry127.com/resources/illustration/the-fastest-man-alive, as accessed on 03/20/2025.
2. Tony Evans Study Bible, Copyright © 2017 by Holman Bible Publishers, Bible Gateway Plus, www.biblegateway.com, as accessed on 03/20/2025.

Going Deeper – A 30-Day Devotional

#15 - A Time for Everything
Read: *Ecclesiastes 3:1-14*

"There is a time for everything, and a season for every activity under the heavens..." **Ecclesiastes 3:1, NIV**

"If you're ever walking the streets of Boston and it starts to rain, look down—you might see something surprising. Boston's City Hall and the nonprofit group Mass Poetry are "slowly bringing secret art to the streets", through a combination of stencils, waterproof spray paint, and rainy days. Since the beginning of April, poems have been sprayed with waterproof paint on sidewalks throughout the city. When the sidewalk is dry, the words are invisible; but when the sidewalk is wet, a piece of art suddenly appears. For many people, a rainy day isn't an ideal day – but who knows what beautiful things a person might miss if it hadn't been for the rain?" **1**

In life, seasons come, and seasons go. We cling tightly to some of them and refuse to move on to new ones. In others, we rush to move on as quickly as possible to a more comfortable situation. But we do not have very much say-so when they change. However, we do know that God has power over our seasons in life, regardless of how long they last.

Big Idea: *Every season in life, both good and bad, is sovereignly ordained by God and is needed to receive God's best for us.*

Notice how verse 1 says, *"There is a time for everything, and a season for every activity under the heavens..."* Some versions use the phrase *"appointed times"*

Going Deeper – A 30-Day Devotional

(NASB), which implies that someone other than us is doing the appointing. And we know from the rest of Scripture that person is God Himself.

Everything that happens to us can be traced back to God's sovereign hand. Absolutely nothing comes into our lives without either God being the originator, or without God allowing it. For some, this can be bad news. If a person is prideful and needs to take credit for the outcome or is uncomfortable trusting God without knowing why He allows the bad seasons, this passage is far from encouraging. But for those of us who choose submission and can rest in the promise that God will *"...cause all things to work together for the good of those who love him,"* (Romans 8:28, NIV) this passage is comforting to hear.

Not only are all seasons, good and bad, ordained by God, but they are fully needed as well. Both highs and lows are important for every person; we cannot have one without the other. Verses 2-8 list *"A time for"* twenty-eight common events that many people go through in life. Most often, it's easier to welcome the good events identified in this list, and it's a lot easier to ignore or avoid the rough times. However, God uses both to accomplish His purposes in each person.

––––––––––––––––

Insight: *Every season in life should cause us to fear God and develop a deep, healthy*
reverence for Him. Regardless of where we are in life, God is always worthy of our respect, honor, and reverence.

––––––––––––––––

So, what are **we** supposed to do? If God has appointed every season of our lives, and is using them to accomplish His purposes in us, how are we to respond? The answer is this: we should learn to be content with whatever God has given us. Look again at verses 12-13: *"I know that there is nothing better for people than to be happy and to do good while they live. That each of them may eat and drink and find satisfaction in all their toil—this is the gift of God."* (NIV)

To clarify, I want to say that these verses do not imply that we shouldn't aspire to better things in life. Or that we should accept everything that comes our way, even if others are treating us unfairly or unjustly. What it is saying is that we should learn to make the most of our everyday routines that we take for granted

Going Deeper – A 30-Day Devotional

sometimes. Philippians 4:12-13 says this: *"I know what it is to be in need, and I know what it is to have plenty. I have learned the secret of being content in any and every situation, whether well fed or hungry, whether living in plenty or in want. I can do all this through him who gives me strength."* (NIV) We should be people who learn to be content with where God has us for that specific reason.

_____

Challenge: *What season of life am I in right now? How can I learn to fear God and be content where I am?*

Pray: *Thanking God for both the good and tough times He has ordained and asking Him to help me be content....*

_____

Going Deeper:

Regarding Ecclesiastes 3, the **Jamieson, Fausset, & Brown Bible Commentary** says the following: *"Earthly pursuits are no doubt lawful in their proper time and order (Ecc 3:1-8), but unprofitable when out of time and place; as for instance, when pursued as the solid and chief*

good (Ecc 3:9, 10); whereas God makes everything beautiful in its season, which man obscurely comprehends (Ecc 3:11). God allows man to enjoy moderately and virtuously His earthly gifts (Ecc 3:12, 13). What consoles us amidst the instability of earthly blessings is, God's counsels are immutable (Ecc 3:14)." **2**

_____

Devotion written by Pastor Frank & Samuel Gervasi

_____

1.   Preaching Today, https://www.preachingtoday.com/illustrations/2016/may/bostons-secret-street-art.html, as accessed on 03/20/2025.
2.   Jamieson, Fausset, & Brown Bible Commentary, 1971, Bible Gateway Plus, www.biblegateway.com, as accessed on 03/20/2025.

Going Deeper – A 30-Day Devotional

Going Deeper – A 30-Day Devotional

#16 - A King Disgraced
Read: *Matthew 27:27-50*

"About three in the afternoon Jesus cried out in a loud voice, 'Eli, Eli, lema sebachthani?' (which means 'My God, my God, why have you forsaken me?')"
Matthew 27:46, NIV

One of the most infamous personalities of the late nineteenth century was Marie Antoinette, queen of France. While her nation was in economic crisis and her people starving, Marie Antoinette was known for her opulent and luxurious lifestyle. She regularly held balls and banquets at the royal palace and was a generous patron to many composers and musicians. She was an avid gambler, often playing to excess, both losing and winning large sums, to such an extent that the King became worried and banned some of the riskier games that were swallowing up entire fortunes. And it has been rumored that when told that the people of Paris had no bread, Queen Marie responded, "Then let them have cake." *1* This queen knew how to get the most out of her royal position.

While Marie Antoinette represents an extreme, many kings and queens have been known to enjoy the luxuries of royalty, whether that be expensive goods, the praise of their people, or the obedience of their every command. In Matthew 27, we are presented with a King – the King of Kings, in fact. But this King doesn't seem to demand the luxuries of His position. Instead, He bears undeserved abuse and mistreatment at the hands of His subjects to change the course of human history forever.

Going Deeper – A 30-Day Devotional

Big Idea: *Christ our King suffered the ridicule of man and the abandonment of the Father that we might receive the forgiveness of God.*

Jesus's kingship is acknowledged in our text – but in the context of mocking and scorn. Initially, the guards mock Him in verses 28-29: *"They stripped him and put a scarlet robe on him and then twisted together a crown of thorns and set it on his head. They put a staff in his right hand. Then they knelt in front of him and mocked him. 'Hail, king of the Jews!' they said."*

Next, the crowds at His crucifixion join in, as we see in verse 42: *"'He saved others,' they said, 'but he can't save himself! He's the king of Israel! Let him come down from the cross, and we will believe in him.'"* (NIV) Even the sign above Jesus's head – THIS IS JESUS, KING OF THE JEWS – has a tone of mockery in it. Jesus, the King of the Universe, humbled Himself beyond belief for the sake of the very people who ridiculed Him.

Insight: *Christ our King died a shameful death – crucified as a common criminal. He humbled Himself and took on the judgment we deserved, so that we could be set free.*

But out of everything that Jesus endured, the worst was not the rejection of the people, but the rejection of the Father – the One who had sent Him. Verses 45-46 say, *"From noon until three in afternoon darkness came over all the land. About three in the afternoon Jesus cried out in a loud voice, 'Eli, Eli, lema sebachthani?' (which means 'My God, my God, why have you forsaken me?')"* God the Father had to turn His back on Christ, because for that time, the sins of the world were put upon Him. 2 Corinthians 5:21 describes it like this: *"He made Him who knew no sin to be sin on our behalf, so that we might become the righteousness of God in Him."* (NASB)

Jesus's ridicule and suffering does end in verse 50: *"And when Jesus had cried out again in a loud voice, he gave up his spirit."* (NIV) Why is this important for us? Because through all this mistreatment Jesus received, and through the offering of His life, death had been conquered! The spotless Lamb, who has taken away the

Going Deeper – A 30-Day Devotional

sins of the sins of the world, paid the ultimate price for a lost humanity. Christ made an acceptable sacrifice to cover our sins once and for all, and to reconcile us to God the Father. Because Jesus endured the ridicule of people and the rejection of the Father, He made a way to restore our relationship with God. And that is why He is worthy of being called the King of Kings.

———————

Challenge: *Do I understand and appreciate what Jesus did at the cross? How can I live in gratitude today?*

Pray: *Thanking God for the humiliation He endured for me to be forgiven…*

———————

Going Deeper:

Verse 34 tells us that the Roman soldiers offered Jesus wine mixed with gall. Some versions use the word myrrh instead of gall. Myrrh, or gall, was a spice derived from plants native to the Arabian desert and parts of Africa. Wine with myrrh was sometimes given to crucifixion victims to deaden the pain, and the Roman soldiers offered it to Jesus, seemingly out of pity. This occurred to fulfill the prophecy of Psalm 69:21: *"They put gall in my food and gave me vinegar for my thirst."* Verse 35 adds that the soldiers gambled for Jesus' clothes, in fulfillment of the prophecy found in Psalm 22:18: *"They divide my clothes among them and cast lots for my garment."*

———————

Devotion written by Pastor Frank & Samuel Gervasi

1. Adapted from https://en.chateauversailles.fr/discover/history/great-characters/marie antoinette#a-queen-at-the-court, as accessed on 03/20/2025

#17 - Benefits of a Thankful/Joyful Spirit
Read: *Philippians 1:3-11*

"I thank my God every time I remember you. 4 In all my prayers for all of you, I always pray with joy."
Philippians 1:3-4, NIV

In her book, *The Hiding Place*, "Corrie Ten Boom relates an incident that taught her to be thankful for things we normally would not be thankful for. She and her sister, Betsy, prisoners of the Nazis, had just been transferred to the worst prison camp they had seen yet, Ravensbrück. Upon entering the barracks, they found them extremely overcrowded and infested with fleas. Their Scripture reading from their smuggled Bible that morning........had reminded them to rejoice always, pray constantly, and give thanks in all circumstances. Betsy told Corrie to stop and thank the Lord for every detail of their new living quarters. Corrie at first flatly refused to give thanks for the fleas, but Betsy persisted. Corrie finally agreed to somehow thank God for even the fleas. During the months spent at that camp, they were surprised to find how openly they could hold Bible study and prayer meetings in their barrack without guard interference. Several months later they learned that the guards would not enter the barracks because of the fleas." *1*

Thankfulness produces much in a person's life seeing good even when circumstances don't warrant joyfulness.

Big Idea: *A Thankful and Joyful Spirit Will Produce Spiritual Fruit and Lead to Wanting the Best in Others.*

A thankful mindset will lead to wanting the best in others-especially those we're close to. Because it reveals something important about a person who is thankful and joyful, that the child of God who's walking in the Spirit and finding their joy in Christ, and that they want to see good things in the life of others. Which is exactly what the Apostle Paul wanted for the church in Philippi. In fact, in vv. 7-8 of today's passage he says, *"It is right for me to feel this way about all of you, since I have you in my heart and, whether I am in chains or defending and confirming the gospel, all of you share in God's grace with me. 8 God can testify how I long for all of you with the affection of Christ Jesus."* NIV

I found myself thinking that what the Apostle prayed for the church at Philippi is not really one that is common for the average person. However, for the Apostle Paul and the church at Philippi in Asia, it's understandable. Because this was said to be a church plant that was ---along with friends of his-- from his second missionary journey. And it was also the first Christian church established in Europe. So, he had a deep connection and affection for them, and he wanted to see the best also.

Insight: A Joyful and Thankful Spirit Should Produce Fruit in Ourselves but Also Those Around Us

---

Additionally, if you look at vv. 9-10 some of the Apostle Paul's desire was being shown because it says: *"And this is my prayer: that your love may abound more and more in knowledge and depth of insight, 10 so that you may be able to discern what is best and may be pure and blameless for the day of Christ."* First, was growth in love which is an increasing *"brotherly love"* for each other, and those around them. But not just a little bit, because the idea behind the word is this: "*to exceed a fixed number of measures, to be left over and above a certain number or measure."***2** Next, was growth in knowledge. Love is more than this ooey-gooey, mushy feeling of affection for someone. Love should always be based on truth. The idea here is *love that is correct and precise.* Then also the Apostle Paul mentions growth in insight. That the church at Philippi would grow in discernment. Which implies *"perception, not only by the senses but by intellect."* **2** So, basically, that they would grow in love, while using all their senses. Billy Graham notes that: *"A spirit of thankfulness is one of the most distinctive marks of a Christian whose heart is attuned to the Lord."* **3**

Going Deeper – A 30-Day Devotional

Challenge: *How grateful am I today for those that God has put in my life? How can I pray for those close to me?*

Pray: *Asking God to help me grow in Thankfulness and Joy...*

Going Deeper:

Joyfulness and Thankfulness are traits and mindsets that can help a person in ways that are unexpected. In fact, the Apostle Paul wrote the letter to the church in Philippi at a time when joy was not normally seen. The Apostle Paul was under house arrest when he wrote this letter. As well as several other letters and epistles known as his Prison Epistles. Embarrassment may have been felt and seen because people in the Roman World viewed incarceration as shameful.

The **Zondervan Cultural Backgrounds Study Bible** notes: *"1:7 'I have you in my heart.' Letters between friends often emphasized that each shared the other's sorrows. Paul's defense and vindication for the gospel would also have relevance for their security (see note on v. 25).' I am in chains.' Most people were ashamed to be associated with anyone chained or in custody of the Roman government. This might be particularly the case in Philippi, which emphasized its close ties with Rome, and where Paul had already been publicly charged with undermining order and the Roman customs of which Philippi was particularly proud (Ac 16:20 – 22)."* **4**

Devotion written by Pastor Frank & Samuel Gervasi

1. The Hiding Place, Chosen Books, 1971
2. Interlinear Bible, https://www.biblestudytools.com, as accessed on 10/04/2024)
3. Goodreads, www.goodreads.com, as accessed on 03/20/2025.
4. Zondervan Cultural Study Bible, Bible Gateway Plus, www.biblegateway.com, as accessed on 03/20/2025.

Going Deeper – A 30-Day Devotional

#18 - Word to the Wise
Read: *1 Corinthians 2:1-8*

"My message and my preaching were not with wise and persuasive words, but with a demonstration of the Spirit's power, so that your faith might not rest on human wisdom, but on God's power." ***1 Corinthians 2:4-5, NIV***

In 2004, a painting by Anna Mary Robertson, better known as Grandma Moses, was brought to the Antiques Roadshow for appraisal. Born before the Civil War, Robertson did not take up painting until late in her life. Her primitive style eventually became extremely popular, and her work commanded a high price. The man who brought the painting to be evaluated had lived nearby and his mother was a friend of Grandma Moses. He said, *"She was just a wonderful friend of the family. And she would let my mother buy these paintings, which she thought had relatively little value. I guess my mother did, too. She probably bought eight or ten paintings in all, and my guess would be for perhaps under ten dollars each." 1* The painting that was bought for around $10 was appraised as being worth $60,000!

Sometimes, the things God reveals in His Word to be wisdom seem like foolishness to the world. We value something of great worth as of little worth at all, because God's commands seem extreme, make us uncomfortable, or even defy common sense. But because God is the origin of all wisdom, the wisdom He has revealed in Christ will always prove superior to the wisdom that culture endorses.

Going Deeper – A 30-Day Devotional

Big Idea: *Jesus is the center and starting point of wisdom, so we should begin with Him if we want to acquire it.*

Notice from our passage that this wisdom with which the Apostle Paul presented the Gospel to the Corinthians was frowned upon by the wisdom of that time: *"We do, however, speak a message of wisdom among the mature, **but not the wisdom of this age** or of the rulers of this age who are coming to nothing."* (NIV, emphasis added)

The *"wisdom of this age"* is simply a person's understanding of God without the help of the Holy Spirit. Think about how the human mind is so easily affected by self-deception; it's easy to convince ourselves that some idea or decision is right, only to end up being wrong. Instead, the Apostle Paul relied on the wisdom of God, *"a mystery that has been hidden and that God destined for our glory before time began,"* (v. 7, NIV).

Insight: *The work of the Holy Spirit is the wisdom of God, and we can trust how that wisdom is manifested and revealed to us through Him.*

Why do we trust in the wisdom of God rather than the wisdom of man? Because Christ is the center of true wisdom. Since God is the creator and origin of all good things, including wisdom, we cannot experience the full extent of it without Jesus as our foundation and starting point. The Apostle Paul *"resolved to know nothing...except Jesus Christ and him crucified."* Paul understood that who Christ is and what He taught was all that was needed, and that the wisdom of the world could not compare. And the same is true for us.

Proverbs 1:7 says this: *"The fear of the LORD is the beginning of knowledge, but fools despise wisdom and instruction."* May Jesus be our starting point today.

Challenge: *Where do I look for wisdom? How can I grow in the wisdom of God?*

Going Deeper – A 30-Day Devotional

Pray: _Asking God to help me make Him my starting point for wisdom, and choosing to obey Him even when I don't understand..._

_____

Going Deeper:

In the **Moody Bible Commentary,** Michael G. Vanlaningham points out how the wisdom found in Christ is available to all who believe in Him: _"**Mature** (v. 6) refers to all believers, not to a few who are insightful. It is possible that by the word **mature** Paul means "mature or spiritual Christians" as opposed to carnal believers, but there are only two categories of people found in 2:1-14, namely those who are purely secular...and those who are Christians (see the many first-person pronouns and verbs found [in the passage] here). In addition, it is highly unlikely that Paul would withhold spiritual truths related to Christ from immature believers. **Mature** here is the term he used for the category of all those who believe in Jesus Christ vis-à-vis the world." **2**

_____

Devotion written by Pastor Frank & Samuel Gervasi

_____

1.   Antiques Road Show, https://www.pbs.org/show/antiques-roadshow, as accessed on 03/20/2025.
2.   Moody Bible Commentary, Moody Publishers, Chicago, 2014

Going Deeper – A 30-Day Devotional

#19 - Biblical Household Submission
Read: *Ephesians 5:21-6:4*

_____

"Submit to one another out of reverence for Christ." **Ephesians 5:21, NIV**

_____

Seatbelts can be a hassle. Some people just don't want to be bothered even when the law requires them to buckle up. According to the Associated Press, a New Zealander named Ivan Segedin took it to an extreme.

"The police ticketed him 32 times over five years for failing to use his seat belt. Even though this was costing him a lot of money, Segedin refused to buckle up. Finally, instead of obeying the law, the man decided to rely on deception. He made a fake seat belt that would hang over his shoulder and made it appear that he was wearing a seat belt when he was not. His trick worked for a while. Then, he had a head-on collision. He was thrown forward onto the steering wheel and killed." **1**

The choices we make can have serious consequences. God has spelled out standards for the structures of families in the Bible also to assure minimal problems.

_____

Big Idea: *Families Have Responsibility to Each Other Member of that Household*

_____

Going Deeper – A 30-Day Devotional

All families will have an important characteristic, evident in their structure. Especially, if they are to be successful, and bring forth fruit, that's consistent with God's plan for them. If each person in a family does not grasp this structure, it won't have a sound foundation to stand on or be successful.

In today's passage the Apostle Paul, in his letter to the church at Ephesus, was giving biblical standards for Christian households.

In v. 21 he says: *"Submit to one another out of reverence for Christ."* Giving us a two-part standard that is important. First, this is the idea of submission. And from a grammatical standpoint, it means literally to: *"arrange under, to subordinate."* However, it's also used as a Greek military term meaning: *"to arrange [troop divisions] in a military fashion under the command of a leader." 2*

Additionally, submission had a third usage in non-military way: *"a voluntary attitude of giving in, cooperating, assuming responsibility, and carrying a burden."* *2* So, in essence the Apostle Paul was implying that families were biblically structured in that way. With each having clearly defined roles and expectations in a particular order.

_____

Insight: *A Christian Family Ultimately Has a Responsibility Before Christ, Himself.*

_____

In addition to that though, the second aspect of submission is really rooted in the why we're supposed to submit to one another. And that is because of Christ Himself! If we look at the second part of v. 21, he says: *"Out of reverence for Christ."* With part of that, acknowledging that Christ is giving us the best way to live successfully as families. Following the patterns set forth in the Bible, including this passage today. *How can a family function properly if everyone has different goals and are moving in different directions?*

_____

Challenge: *How can we be the best family member where God has placed us? Am I submitting in reverence of Christ?*

Going Deeper – A 30-Day Devotional

Pray: *Asking God to help me be the best family member I can be, for the sake of my family and Christ...*

Going Deeper:

Whatever our role is in the family, we should understand submission and yield to each other for its smooth functioning. The **NKJV Wiersbe Study Bible** says:

"It is only through the power of the Holy Spirit that we can walk in harmony.....the unity of the people of God that Paul described (4:1–16) must be translated into daily living if we are to enjoy the harmony that is a foretaste of heaven on earth. If our homes are to be a heaven on earth, then we must be controlled by the Holy Spirit." 3

Devotion written by Pastor Frank & Samuel Gervasi

---

1.   https://www.sermoncentral.comhttps//www.sermoncentral.com/sermon-illustrations/70702/fake-seatbelts-and-submission-by-sermon-central, as accessed on 10/13/2024)
2.   Interlinear Bible, biblestudytools.com, as accessed on 03/20/2025.
3.   NKJV Wiersbe Bible, Copyright 2021, Thomas Nelson.

Going Deeper – A 30-Day Devotional

#20 - Letting Go
Read: *Ephesians 5:22-24*

"Wives, submit yourselves to your own husbands as you do to the Lord."
Ephesians 5:22, NIV

"According to the Associated Press, on December 14, 1996, a 763-foot grain freighter was heading down the Mississippi at New Orleans, Louisiana, when it lost control, veered toward the shore, and crashed into a riverside shopping mall. At the time the Riverwalk Mall was crowded with some 1,000 shoppers, and 116 people were injured. After investigating the accident for a year, the Coast Guard reported that the freighter had lost control because the engine had shut down. The engine had shut down because of low oil pressure. The oil pressure was low because of a clogged oil filter. And the oil filter was clogged because the ship's crew had failed to maintain the engine properly." 1

Sometimes, if something is managed and run in a way it wasn't designed to be, the smallest mistakes can have disastrous consequences.

Big Idea: *Wives have a responsibility in accordance with God's structure for the family to submit to their husbands' leadership.*

Verses like the kind we read today have become taboo in modern culture. And to an extent, it's easy to see why. This passage has given birth to wrong teaching, selfish desires for control, and resistance to the principle at hand. However, just because this passage has been misunderstood, does not cancel out or nullify God's roles for the Christian household.

Going Deeper – A 30-Day Devotional

Perhaps the qualifier in verse 22 – "*...as you do to the Lord,*" – helps us understand submission as God intended it. When we submit to Christ, He doesn't take advantage of us. He doesn't treat us like an insignificant nobody. He doesn't treat us as His slaves. Rather, we are of infinite value to God, and the purpose of Jesus' life, ministry, and death was "*...it is for **freedom** that Christ has set you free.*" (Galatians 5:1, NIV; emphasis added)

Insight: **Submission is to be extensive and complete. In the end, the final direction for the family unit should be the direction the husband leads toward.**

So, what is biblical submission? Biblical submission is viewing the husband as responsible and acting accordingly. In the end, each husband and father will give account for the kind of stewards they were of their families on earth. Husbands should be leading in a way that saves and redeems their families and values them as second only to Christ. And the wife should strengthen and support her husband in fulfilling that role, not working against him.

Challenge: **What is the family role God has for me? How can I grow in fulfilling that role?**

Pray: **Asking God to help me submit and trust His sovereignty in the direction of my family...**

Going Deeper:

The **Dictionary of Bible Themes** defines the word *submission* as follows:

"*A humble attitude where obedience is rendered within a relationship; whether it be to God, authorities or other people at work, in the church, in marriage or in the family.*" **2**

Devotion written by Pastor Frank & Samuel Gervasi

---

1. Taken from https://sermoncentral.com/sermon-illustrations/9589/losing-control-one-mistake-at-a-time-by-john-williams-iii, as accessed on 03/20/2025.
2. Dictionary of Bible Themes, Bible Gateway Plus, www.biblegateway.com, as accessed on 03/20/2025.

Going Deeper – A 30-Day Devotional

#21 - Husbands Leading in Love
Read: *Ephesians 5:25-33*

"Husbands, love your wives, just as Christ loved the church and gave himself up for her." **Ephesians 5:25, NIV**

The idea that we have the ideal spouse has proved popular in our culture. One source said. *"Among young adults in the U.S. A 2011 poll found that 73% of Americans believed in a soulmate, the idea that 'two people are destined to be together,' with fully 80% of those under 30 taking this view. However, for those seeking a soulmate, what matters is emotional skills and the ability to spark romantic or sexual chemistry. These qualities are supposed to put men and women on the path to what they see as the primary goods of marriage: intimacy, self-expression, and self-fulfillment"* **1**

Which may be true with many variables that may make the ideal marriage. Nevertheless, God has spelled out a husband's role clearly giving them guidelines to follow.

Big Idea: *Husbands Have Responsibility to Their Wives, Treating Them with Care and Respect.*

In today's devotion continuing in our family focus we discover a husband's role. In Ephesians 5 where the Apostle Paul was giving further instructions to families, he addresses the husband. Using the strong word "responsibility" that of gives an image of commitment and being deliberate. And commitment and

Going Deeper – A 30-Day Devotional

deliberateness are favorable and dignified treatment, of our spouses. I'm not talking about perfect, or saying that couples don't have their differences, but in the end the treatment is one of respect. In verse 25-27 he says: *"Husbands, love your wives, just as Christ loved the church and gave himself up for her to make her holy, cleansing [a] her by the washing with water through the word, and to present her to himself as a radiant church, without stain or wrinkle or any other blemish, but holy and blameless."* Consider how the Apostle Paul gives us three different examples of what a husband's love for his wife might involve.

First, a *sacrificial love* and one that honors their spouse, with a deep and reverent respect for her. Probably the opposite of what is sometimes seen in our culture. I want to tell you that it irks me when I see people speak about their wives in a negative tone, sharing things about them with coworkers that is demeaning. I've heard people talk about their wives in some disrespectful manner, and I've thought, what are you doing? It's rude plus counter-productive to anything good! Think about the comparison used of *"Christ and the church, holy, spotless, and blameless."*

Second, the Apostle Paul talks about a *respectful love* because here in v. 28, the Bible is saying it's ok to love yourself. *"In this same way, husbands ought to love their wives as their own bodies. He who loves his wife loves himself. After all, no one ever hated their own body, but they feed and care for their body,"* Even though the words invoke a selfish motivation, it's really one of stewardship and taking care of oneself. And, if we're honest we all know how to care for and respect our own bodies. *So, it kind of puts things in perspective, doesn't it?*

Insight: *Husbands Should Be Loving Their Wives with A Sacrificial, Respectful, & Unified Love*

Finally, a *unified love* is one that is working together with your spouse, and you're both moving the family in the direction that is best for your family. Because in verse 31 he says, *"For this reason a man will leave his father and mother and be united to his wife, and the two will become one flesh."* Implying something important like, not what's best for your mother or father, or what they would do. It is your family, and it should be shaped for you both to work. However, that's not to say that you don't have anything to do with them, or parents can't give some valuable insights. Especially since they know their kids and what might help. But

Going Deeper – A 30-Day Devotional

ultimately living your own lives, as husband and wife. The Apostle Paul was cross referencing Genesis 2:24 where God was ordaining marriage in the first place.

––––––––––––––––

Challenge: *Am I loving my wife as Christ did the Church? Or am I treating her as a insignificant doormat?*

Pray: *Asking God to help me show a sacrificial, respectful, & unified love to my wife...*

––––––––––––––––

Going Deeper:

The **NKJV Maxwell Leadership Bible** defines the phrase *leadership in the home* as follows: *"Contrary to what many teach, leadership in the home is not about power or control. Paul asks for mutual submission (Eph. 5:21) and calls husbands to be Christ-figures (5:23–25). And how did Christ lead the church? He provided, taught, wept, healed, and died on a cross. Spiritual leadership means giving up yourself for someone else (5:25). It means assuming responsibility for the health and development of your relationships." 2*

––––––––––––––––

Devotion written by Pastor Frank & Samuel Gervasi

––––––––––––––––

1. Adapted from https://www.preachingtoday.com/illustrations/2024/october/myth-of-perfect-soulmate.html, as accessed on 10/20.2024.
2. NKJV Maxwell Leadership Bible. Copyright © 2002, 2007, 2018 by Maxwell Motivation, Inc.

Going Deeper – A 30-Day Devotional

Going Deeper – A 30-Day Devotional

#22 - The Children's Part
Read: *Ephesians 6:1-4*

"Children, obey your parents in the Lord, for this is right." **Ephesians 6:1, NIV**

Every year, between January 29th and April 15th, people begin the tedious work of filing their taxes. *"One central component of tax season is claiming exemptions from certain chargers. And some of the things people have tried to claim as tax exemptions over the years can be comical from our vantage point. For example, one man tried to soften the blow of paying for his daughter's wedding by inviting a few of his business clients and writing the wedding off as business entertainment. Others, on more than one occasion, have tried to write off their dog or cat as a dependent. Furthermore, one family constructed a doomsday fallout shelter near their home and tried to claim it as preventative medicine. Obviously, all these claims were denied."* **1**

In previous weeks, we have discussed the family roles of both wives and husbands. But some of us are neither. Such people may try to *exempt* themselves from the guidelines given in Ephesians 5-6, like tax exemption. But all of us are children. And, therefore, we all have a role given by God to honor Him in our families.

Big Idea: **Children have a responsibility to obey their parents if they want God's blessing.**

Going Deeper – A 30-Day Devotional

In our passage today, the Apostle Paul addresses the children at Ephesus and their role in a Christian family structure. Verses 1-2 tell us: *"Children, obey your parents in the Lord, for this is right. 'Honor your father and mother' – which is the first commandment with a promise – 'so that it might go well with you and that you might enjoy long life on earth.'"* (NIV) Now, it would be easy to note the phrase *"Obey...**in the Lord**,"* (emphasis added) and attempt to claim another exemption. Not all of us have parents who are "in the Lord". Some of us have parents that do not know God and follow His Word, or else were flawed in their parenting style.

It's important to note that all parents are ordained by God and were chosen by Him to raise us. No one gets to choose their families of origin – that role is reserved for God alone, and He does not make mistakes. We should still obey our parents, because they are older and wiser than we are. They were hand-picked by God to mold us into who He wanted us to become.

Insight: *A person doesn't outgrow obeying his parents when he becomes an adult. All of us, no matter our age, are still called to treat our parents with respect, listen to their advice, and so long as it lines up with Scripture, apply it to our lives.*

Finally, look back at the promise we're given in verse 2 if we obey: *"'...it may go well with you and that you might enjoy long life on earth."* This verse shows us that this is a cause-and-effect relationship. If we submit to God's Word and accept our God-given role in the household, we will get the best results in our families. Whatever role God has given us in the household, we can rest assured that God has a structure and model for how to honor Him in that role. And it will always be the best way!

Challenge: *What is the family role God has for me? How can I grow in fulfilling that role? How can I respect my parents today?*

Pray: *Asking God to help me respect and obey my parents...*

Going Deeper:

Going Deeper – A 30-Day Devotional

In conclusion of our two-week focus on biblical family roles, the **NIV Biblical Theology Study Bible** notes the importance of Christ being the center of our families, and provides the key to applying these verses to our lives: *"After instructing believers how to live worthy of their calling within the community of faith (4:17—5:20), Paul instructs them how to live within the household. The link between these two sections is 5:21; the submission called for in the household instructions **depends on being 'filled with the Spirit'** [emphasis added] (5:18; see note there). These instructions primarily differ from traditional Greco-Roman codes by presenting Christ as the true head of the family. The order within these codes reflects how the Christian household should work out Christ's unity over all things."*

Devotion written by Pastor Frank & Samuel Gervasi

---

1. Adapted from https://turbotax.intuit.com/tax-tips/fun-facts/7-of-the-craziest-illegal-tax-deductions-ever-claimed/L3ZEIWEFZ, as accessed on 03/20/2025.
2. NIV Biblical Theology Study Bible. Copyright © 2019 by Zondervan.
3.

Going Deeper – A 30-Day Devotional

Going Deeper – A 30-Day Devotional

23 - I Promise #1
Read: *Genesis 28:11-15*

"I am with you and will watch over you wherever you go, and I will bring you back to this land. I will not leave you until I have done what I have promised you."
Genesis 28:15, NIV

"One stormy night an elderly couple entered the lobby of a small hotel and asked for a room. The clerk said they were full, and they would probably find so were all the hotels in town. 'But I can't send a fine couple like you out in the rain. Would you be willing to sleep in my room?' The couple hesitated, but the clerk insisted.

The next morning when the man paid his bill, he said, 'You're the kind of man who should be managing the best hotel in the United States. Someday I'll build you one.' The clerk smiled politely. A few years later the clerk received a letter containing an airplane ticket; the letter invited him to visit New York. When the clerk arrived, his host took him to the corner of 5th Avenue and 34th Street, where there stood a magnificent new building. 'That,' explained the man, "is the hotel I have built for you to manage.'" The elderly man had not forgotten the promise he had given to the clerk. *"The name of the clerk was William Waldorf Astor, and the hotel was the original Waldorf-Astoria."* **1**

Today, our devotion series begins regarding the life of Jacob. Looking at the promises of God.

Going Deeper – A 30-Day Devotional

Big Idea: *God has to make the promise first before we can claim it as our own.*

_____

In our passage today, we see an important promise of God. Given specifically to Jacob and his descendants. Nevertheless, God makes promises to his children often in life. However, a person can't always just claim every promise made in Scripture to our own situation. Even though people do it often, it's not necessarily a good thing. Because some are specific to a group or to an individual in Scripture most often, even though we may have common things that we can apply.

In today's reading the encounter and promise was for Jacob, while he was on his journey we know from the text that he stops for the night being tired. And then we see in v. 11 *"that he picks up a stone to lay his head on."* Which may not have been the most comfortable surroundings. However, don't forget that Jacob fled in haste. *It sometimes seems that God chooses the times we are most receptive to hear Him.*

Also, Jacob encounters God in a dream that was to change his life from that point forward. In v. 12 it says: *"He had a dream in which he saw a stairway resting on the Earth, with its top reaching to heaven. And the angels of God were ascending and descending on it."*

Now, in this passage we should look at some background information that can help us. Because what was going on is that Jacob had just fled from his home --- and had run to get away from his brother Esau ---in fear for his life.

If you know the story Jacob had done some dishonest and deceitful things in his life. In fact, he was called *the Deceiver* (Genesis 25:26,) which was characteristic of his nature at that time. Because he had deceived his brother Esau and Isaac for some important things namely two. His birthright and Isaac's blessing both, which were reserved for the older son and not the youngest, *(Genesis 25:28-34.)* Now the birthright was taken over a bowl of stew that Esau wanted and gave it up willingly to Jacob, after returning from hunting all day. And the blessing from Isaac was taken by pretending to be Esau and tricking their elderly father whose sight had gone bad. *(Genesis 27)* And, when Esau finds out what had happened, he was upset and Jacob flees for Haran to live with an uncle, which brings us to our current story.

But then he makes a powerful promise to Jacob, doesn't He? *"I am the LORD, the God of your father Abraham and the God of Isaac."* The same promises that he made earlier to both individuals Abraham and Isaac. And he was reaffirming it again here. And the promise itself was reserved for their descendants because it was a promise for specific land that is still disputed to this day.

Insight: If God has made us a promise, we should apply it our lives the best we can....

Finally, God will do whatever it takes to get our attention in life. Maybe, for some major decision that we are on the brink of making. Maybe, it's about a new job that you've been seeking Him about, ---or a relationship you find yourself in and don't know how to proceed with it. If that's your goal in the first place. Or maybe it's about a new area of your life that's about to change, and He really wants to get your attention.

Whatever God promises He will make sure it happens. And is contingent on God seeing it through, not us. *Charles Stanley* says that: *"God will always stay with us and keep all His promises to us, even when we go through the storms of life. When we wonder if He's there, He is!"* **2**

<u>Challenge:</u>   *What is the promise God has for me? How can I apply it best to my situation?*

<u>Pray:</u>   *Asking God to help us trust fully in His promises always...*

Going Deeper:

The **NIV Grace and Truth Study Bible** regarding Genesis 28:10–17: *"The author backtracks to describe a particular stopover on Jacob's journey from Beersheba to Harran. About two to three days into his journey, Jacob stops at a place called Luz, located about 60 miles from Beersheba. Ironically, the first time Jacob will truly wake up is when he goes to sleep, for it is in the quietness of inactivity that he hears God. This is the second dream in the Bible in which someone explicitly*

Going Deeper – A 30-Day Devotional

experiences a revelation from God (cf. 20:3). Jacob dreams of a stairway to heaven on which angels descend and ascend, taking their directions from the Lord, who stands at the top of the staircase. The stairway is more like a ramp than a ladder, resembling the tower of Babel structure, which rebellious humans constructed to unite heaven to earth. In an act of grace, God himself gives the Abrahamic promise directly to Jacob. God now for the first time calls himself not only the God of Abraham but also the God of Isaac. Despite everything, he will also be Jacob's God. When Jacob awakens, awe overwhelms him. The words translated "afraid" and "awesome" (28:17) come from the same Hebrew word meaning fear. Together they capture the awe-inspiring experience of a creature coming into the presence of its Creator. Jacob responds that this place is significant because it is none other than the house of God ("Bethel") and the gateway of heaven, the place where heaven and earth are united. Jesus will eventually serve as such a bridge between heaven and earth (Jn 1:51), finally bringing the Bible's storyline into complete unity (Rev 21:3)." **3**

Devotion written by Pastor Frank & Samuel Gervasi

---

1. www.sermoncentral.com/sermonillustrations/77498/astor-s-promise-by-gordon-curley, as accessed on 10/27/2024.
2. Charles Stanley Life Application Bible, Bible Gateway Plus, www.biblegateway.com, as accessed on 03/20/2025.
3. NIV Grace & Truth Bible, Bible Gateway Plus, www.biblegateway.com, as accessed on 03/20/2025.

Going Deeper – A 30-Day Devotional

#24 - I Promise #2
Read: *Genesis 28:13-17*

"He was afraid and said, 'How awesome is this place! This is none other than the house of God; this is the gate of heaven.'" **Genesis 28:17, NIV**

There's a story about "a nurse living in the UK. At the healthcare facility where she works there is one patient with dementia who the nurse eats lunch with daily. *The only problem is she's always afraid I won't come back. That I will forget her,* Elizabeth said.....So, one day, Elizabeth wrote this patient a note, promising that she would remember to have lunch with her and not forget her. The patient took this note and placed it in her room. And in the days and weeks that followed, this patient would look at the note and remember the promise that was made if she forgot and began to worry." **1**

Last Sunday, we began our focus on the life of Jacob, and God's promises to him. Today, we will see the importance of remembering God's promises, just like the elderly woman who looked at the note and remembered the promise made to her.

Big Idea: *Sometimes We Must Reflect on God's Promises to Further Solidify Them in our Hearts.*

In verses 16 and 17, we see Jacob awake from his vision of the ladder, in which God had promised to bless Jacob and his descendants and be with him. And we

Going Deeper – A 30-Day Devotional

can obviously see that this whole sequence of events has Jacob a little freaked out: *"When Jacob awoke from his sleep, he thought, 'Surely the LORD is in this place, and I was not aware of it.' **He was afraid...**"* (Genesis 28:16-17a, NIV; emphasis added)

The word *afraid* is interesting and catches our attention, because it carries with it a few different meanings. It implies a combination of fright and alarm, and reverential fear. This combination shows us that Jacob was in full realization that the God of the universe, and the God of his own ancestors, had spoken directly to him.

––––––––––––

Insight: **God is omnipresent – He is always everywhere, and this should lead us to be more in awe of him and trust Him even more to fulfill His promises to us.**

––––––––––––

Some people have described these verses as Jacob's conversion experience – when he finally stops running from God's plan for His life and begins to serve the Lord as his own God. Almost all of us can remember the day of our own conversion, and the way it causes us to reflect on what God has done and how He has spoken to us.

Reflecting on and realizing who God is helps us to believe in the promises He makes, and remembering what He has done in the past helps us to keep believing when the waiting gets long. Jacob did these things, and it helped him understand the promise God had given him. And we should do the same thing.

Josh McDowell said this: *"Knowing that God is faithful, it really helps me to not be captivated by worry. But knowing that He will do what He has said. He will cause it to happen, whatever He has promised, thinking about it, then it causes me to be less involved in worrying about a situation." **2***

––––––––––––

Challenge: **Which promises of God do I need to reflect on? What promises do I need to remember?**

Going Deeper – A 30-Day Devotional

Pray: Asking God to help me remember His promises and solidify them in my mind...

Going Deeper:

The **Wycliffe Bible Dictionary** defines the word *promise* as follows: *"While referring occasionally to a man's word. The characteristic use of 'promise' in Scripture is concerning what God declares he will bring to pass...God's first great promise to man is in Genesis 3:15 inaugurating the succession which, in growing clarity and detail right down to the annunciation, tells of the coming Messiah-Deliverer. A wide range of promises is connected more or less directly with this central promise, including the new covenant (Jer 31:31-34), the outpouring of the Spirit (Joel 2:28 f.), the restoration of Israel (Deut 30:1-5), and ultimately, new heavens and new earth (Isa 65:17; 66:22)...The technical term **epangelia** , then, designates God's whole gracious commitment, expressed especially to Abraham [and passed on to Jacob], to perform His full redemptive work in Messiah, in whom 'all the promises of God are yea and amen' (II Cor 1:20)."* **3**

Devotion written by Pastor Frank & Samuel Gervasi

---

1. Adapted from https://becauseisaidiwould.org/i-will-come-back-for-lunch/; as accessed on 10/29/24.
2. Josh McDowell, https://www.goodreads.com/author/quotes/4314.Josh_McDowell, as accessed on 10/29/2024.
3. Wycliffe Bible Dictionary, by Charles F. Pfeiffer, Howard F. Vos, and John Rea. Copyright © 1999 by Hendrickson Publishers. All rights reserved.

Going Deeper – A 30-Day Devotional

#25 - Memorials in Context
Read: *Genesis 28:16-19*

"He called that place Bethel, though the city used to be called Luz.'" **Genesis 28:19, NIV**

"Arlington National Cemetery, is the U.S. national burial ground in Arlington County, Virginia, on the Potomac River directly opposite Washington, D.C. The cemetery currently occupies 612 acres. The first soldier buried (May 13, 1864) on the Lee plantation was a Confederate prisoner who had died in a local hospital. Sixty-four other soldiers were also buried that day, including some in the estate's rose garden, and by the end of 1864 more than 7,000 soldiers had been interred. The cemetery subsequently became the burial ground for casualties from all U.S. wars since the American Revolution. Prominent soldiers and civilians have been buried at Arlington ever since serving as a memorial to remember them. " **1**

Recently, we began our focus on the life of Jacob, and God's promises to him. Today, we will see the importance of remembering God's promises, and key encounters people have with Him by using memorials.

Big Idea: *Reminders are helpful—if they lead us to a deeper appreciation of God himself.*

Reminders are alright—if they lead us to a greater reverence of God and draws us closer to Him. Because in essence setting up reminders are ways to memorialize the event itself. Opportunities to think about and replay the encounter in our

Going Deeper – A 30-Day Devotional

minds. And it's a good thing in most cases, if it leads us to a deeper appreciation about the promises *and* God.

In the case of Jacob, he does a couple of important but different things, doesn't he? Look starting in v. 18: *"Early the next morning Jacob took the stone he had placed his head under and set it up as a pillar and poured oil on top of it. He called that place Bethel though the city used to be called Luz."* Notice how he does three different things to help remember as well. First, Jacob used a bridge or tie, something that was from the actual event, like the *"stone" (vv. 17, 18)* that he laid his head on. Probably so that when he saw it, he could recall it even more clearly, and what happened that day.

Second, he also consecrated the place meaning that he set it apart and had a mini ceremony where he could further memorialize it. Because Jacob then *"poured oil on top it." (v. 18)* Which obviously *wasn't* doing it for prayer purposes but just another way that would cause him to remember the event further.

Then lastly, renames the location, which was giving it that final, new identification. And the name itself *"Bethel"* means *"House of God." (v. 19),* which remained for many years in Israel with that name.

Insight: Memorials are good but should never replace God or a person's relationship with God. In and of themselves they hold nothing unique, other than reflection.

However, if you noticed I said memorials are good in *some* cases. However, not in all instances, because they can have an undesired result also, especially, as they relate to matters of faith. That's because we want to be cautious that they don't replace God, going to Him in prayer, or that personal one-on-one time. Also, someone should be careful not to believe the memorial has some special power in and of itself. Like a statue or something like that, because they should cause us to deeper appreciation of the event or promise but not replace it. C.S. Lewis says: *"A pleasure is full grown only when it is remembering. You are speaking...as if pleasure were one thing and memory another. It is all one thing." 2*

Going Deeper – A 30-Day Devotional

Challenge: What memorials are important for me to reflect on God? Which ones have I allowed to replace my time with Him?

Pray: Asking God, to help us remember your goodness to us always...

_____

Going Deeper:

The **NIV Application Commentary** comments on Genesis 28:12-16 as follows: *"When Jacob awakes, he has two responses. (1) He recognizes the nature of the place, which involves three steps. (a) He identifies the sacredness of the spot. Portals were associated with sacred space. It has already been noted that the ziggurats, representing portals, were constructed next to temples, which demarcated sacred space. Since Jacob has seen a portal here, he identifies the space as sacred space, a house of God. This house of God is at the earth end of the portal, whereas the other end of the portal is the gate of heaven. In Mesopotamian literature, the stairway led to the gate of the gods, and Jacob is thinking in those same terms. (b) Jacob sets up the stone as a pillar. Sacred pillars and standing stones are familiar in the religious environment of the ancient world. Archaeologists have found them in a variety of cultic settings dating from the fourth millennium to the first. They can be either natural or carved, inscribed or plain. The Canaanites used them (e.g., at the high place at Gezer), and they were found at the Israelite cultic installation at Arad. Anointing the pillar constitutes its dedication. Some of the standing stones that have been found include basins at their base for libations.* These stones are sometimes understood as the dwelling places of deity (houses of god)."* **3**

_____

Devotion written by Pastor Frank & Samuel Gervasi

_____

1. Adapted from https://www.britannica.com/place/Arlington-National-Cemetery; as accessed on 10/31/ 2024.
2. AZ Quotes, https://www.azquotes.com/quote/381374, as accessed on 10/31/2024.
3. NIV Application Commentary, Genesis, John Walton, Zondervan Academic 10/01/2000.

Going Deeper – A 30-Day Devotional

#26 - A Commitment of His Own
Read: *Genesis 28:20-22*

"'...then the LORD will be my God...'" **Genesis 28:21b, NIV**

One of the most important parts of a wedding ceremony is the "I do's", where each of the members of that marriage promise to love and stand by the other as a promise before God. To commemorate this pledge, the members of the marriage wear a ring on their fingers, to remind themselves of the commitment they are making. In our devotion today, we conclude our focus on Jacob's encounter with God at Bethel. And we will see how the promises God had made prompts Jacob to respond with a promise of his own.

Big Idea: *God's Promises Should Lead Us to Commitment and Relationship.*

In verse 20, we see that *"Then Jacob made a vow..."*. In this resolution, Jacob expresses his desire to serve God and follow Him if God will look after Jacob and keep the promises He had made in the vision. Our passage lists five small components of this promise Jacob makes before God. First, he asks God for provision. Remember that Jacob fled his home abruptly to escape his brother Esau's retaliation, so Jacob was declaring his dependence on the Lord to supply necessities like food and clothing. Jacob also asks for God's protection as he traveled alone through the wilderness. Subsequently, Jacob commits himself to personally serve Yahweh as his own God, as we see in verse 21b: *"'...then the LORD will be **my** God...'"* (NIV; emphasis added). Jacob had personally seen the glory of God, and he wanted in on a personal relationship with this God of promises.

Insight: **God desires to have a personal relationship with each person – for them to be His children and be known by Him. He longs to be in fellowship**

Going Deeper – A 30-Day Devotional

with those who fear Him.

After Jacob commits himself to this personal relationship, he goes a bit further – promising not only to remember the promise God had made to him at Bethel, but also to give of his own treasures and resources as an offering to God: *"...and of all that you give me I will give you a tenth."* (v. 22) God desires for us to be committed to and in relationship with Him. And when He makes a promise to us, we should be moved to commit ourselves to Him in return. Because God is faithful to fulfill each one of His promises.

Challenge: *How do I respond when God makes a promise to me? How can I serve and follow Him in gratitude today?*

Pray: *Asking God to care for me, and help me to serve Him considering His promises...*

Going Deeper:

Zondervan Illustrated Bible Backgrounds Commentary of the Old Testament says: *"Vows in the ancient world generally involved a request made of deity with a promise of a gift in return when the request is fulfilled. The request often concerned protection or provision, and the gift was typically a sacrifice or a donation to the sanctuary of the deity. The details in this chapter conform to that pattern. God has promised protection, provision, and return to the land, so Jacob makes those the condition of his proffered gift: a tithe of all that he acquires during his absence. Wealth and possession in the ancient world were not based on money, so Jacob expects to gain flocks and herds. Though tithes could at times be a form of taxation, this tithe is not imposed on Jacob. Gifts related to vows were usually given to the temple (whether by means of sacrifice or donation), but in this case it will have to be by, sacrifice because donations must be handed over to temple administrators, and there is no formal temple here. Jacob returns to Bethel to fulfill his vow in Genesis 35."* **1**

Devotion written by Pastor Frank & Samuel Gervasi

---

1.   Zondervan Illustrated Bible Backgrounds Commentary of the Old Testament, Copyright © 2002.

Going Deeper – A 30-Day Devotional

#27 - In Focus
Read: *John 5:1-15*

"Do you want to get well?'" John 5:6, NIV

In our devotion today we're beginning a look at prayer. And we'll study a story about a man who needed God's healing. He was an invalid, for a very long time and had tried many times to do what some sick people were used to doing but had a hard time of it. In fact, we'll see some attitudes that are common, especially when it comes to change in people's lives or overcoming obstacles in a particular area of life.

Big Idea: *When trying to overcome obstacles we should pray with focus*

When facing a challenge, we should understand your obstacle (vv. 1-4.) Meaning that if we are going to change in anyway, whether it's a big challenge or a small one, we need to understand what it is fully. Now in the case of the story the challenge was physical healing. But there were obstacles that lie in the mental arena that we're going to look at, as well. The location itself was called "Bethesda", depending on your version. However, v. 2 says, *"Now there is in Jerusalem near the Sheep Gate a pool, which in Aramaic is called Bethesda[a] and which is surrounded by five covered colonnades."*
Some have suggested it means *"House of mercy"*, (unknown). However, it was one that Jesus knew well, because it was the place of the feeding of the 5000. As well as one of the disciples Phillip was from there. But also, in v.2 they mention a sheep gate. So, there was buying and selling of sheep, also a pool for watering sheep, probably the shepherds as well. So, you can kind of picture the surroundings, a little. However, also think about the atmosphere that was present, there were different obstacles. First, were many disabled people: meaning sick people were lying around. In fact, v. 3 says, *"A great number of sick*

Going Deeper – A 30-Day Devotional

people." So, I think it might have been a little depressing, and kind of sad surroundings.

Insight: **Regardless of the obstacle God can bring victory, but we should overcome negative attitudes and show faith by trusting Him fully**

The various levels of need are opportunities to show our faith in God. In today's passage he brings up a couple more. *"Here a great number of disabled people used to lie—the blind, the lame, the paralyzed. 5 One who was there had been an invalid for thirty-eight years.* Not to minimize any physical challenge but the blind was maybe the least dependent on others. Because they can still walk and do some things for themselves. However, the lame may have been only a body part or two not functioning. Nevertheless, the paralyzed were probably the worst of them because this may have been total in nature. Additionally, the length of need was long because v. 5 says, *"he had been invalid for thirty-eight years."*

Regardless of how big or difficult our challenges are in life; we should stay focused because God is able, and we can trust Him fully.

Challenge: **How do we approach the challenges in life? Do we pray with focus or not??**

Pray: **Asking God to give us focus and insight that can help give us faith when we pray...**

Going Deeper:

Zondervan Illustrated Bible Backgrounds Commentary of the Old Testament says: *"A pool . . . called Bethesda (5:2). Public baths were standard in Greco-Roman cities, and people congregated there. A Qumran scroll attests the name of this pool (3Q15 11.12–13), and archaeologists have discovered a pool in this location fitting precisely this description. Although scholars do not all agree on the site of Bethesda (or its exact spelling), many favor a site under the Church of St. Anne in Jerusalem, just north-northeast of the temple. The pools were quite large (like a football field) and roughly twenty feet deep. This site had two twin pools, surrounded by four porches, or porticoes, and one porch (a fifth one) down the middle separating the pools (perhaps separating genders). Although John writes after Jerusalem was destroyed in ad 70, his recollection of the site is accurate."* **1**

Devotion written by Pastor Frank & Samuel Gervasi

---

1.   Zondervan Illustrated Bible Backgrounds Commentary of the Old Testament, Copyright © 2002.

Going Deeper – A 30-Day Devotional

#28 - Pick Up Your Mat
Read: *John 5:5-15*

"At once, the man was healed; he picked up his mat and walked." **John 5:9a, NIV**

Bubble Wrap celebrated its golden anniversary in January of 2010. Although the primary function is to provide cushioned security, *"Bubble Wrap was originally invented for another use: wallpaper. In the late 1950s, a New York City designer was looking for a new type of textured wall covering, but the idea never took off. Inventors Marc Chavannes and Al Fielding envisioned a different application for the bubbly wallpaper, however. They decided to make a change and created an industry with annual revenues of $4 billion. The vision of these two inventors made the difference between success and failure for Bubble Wrap."* **1**

Sometimes, we all come to a point where what we've been doing just isn't working, and we need a change – a transformation, if you will. As Christians, we have access to life-changing power in Christ, but sometimes our own emotions and attitudes can stand in the way.

Big Idea: *When we are seeking transformation in life, we must overcome the negative attitudes and mindsets that come our way.*

Whatever the area we may be seeking change in, we can be sure that there will be people whose dispositions and perspectives will try to hinder the growth we're seeking.

Going Deeper – A 30-Day Devotional

Look at vv. 9b-10 *"The day on which this took place was a Sabbath, and so the Jewish leaders said to the man who had been healed, 'It is the Sabbath; the law forbids you to carry your mat.'"* (NIV) If that is not about the most horrible thing to say to someone who was crippled and then healed! But if we look closer, we can see that the religious leaders weren't the only ones to bring their baggage to this situation – the invalid had his own obstacles too! In verse six, Jesus asks a question that seems ridiculous on the surface: *"Do you want to get well?'"* Isn't it obvious to Jesus that the answer is an adamant "YES!!"? Yet look at the invalid's response to Jesus in v.7: *"I have no one to help me into the pool when the water is stirred. While I am trying to get in, someone else goes ahead of me."* When presented with an opportunity to move forward with transformation in the present, he instead looks to the past and reveals an attitude of thorough discouragement. It seems that he has maybe even given up looking for healing. Maybe Jesus' question wasn't so ridiculous after all.

Insight: *Each person is different – physically, in character, and in mindset. It is important to understand ourselves to understand the exact attitudes that we will have to overcome.*

Even today, we as Christians bring our negative mindsets to the table when God wants to do something great in our lives. Some of us bring a calloused heart that is suspicious and untrusting of God because of past trials. Some of us bring a fearful outlook that looks more at the obstacles than at God's power and so refuses to step out of the boat. Some of us bring a toxic negativity, that refuses to take joy in God's blessings and always expects the worst – because of a fear of being let down. God desires for us to lay down these negative attitudes – to trust Him fully and allow His life-changing power to do its work. This is not to say that because we have faith, we will always receive the desired outcome; but it is to say that when we trust God, the unhindered transformation He brings will always be for our best.

In the end, the invalid at the pool was healed that day, and Jesus completely changed his life. We, too, may need God's transformation in some area of our lives. Let's lay down those attitudes and mindsets that hinder us and choose instead to trust and surrender to Him.

_____

<u>Challenge:</u>   *What are some attitudes that don't bring God glory? How can I overcome them and choose to trust today?*

<u>Pray:</u>   *Asking God to help me trust no matter the obstacles I face...*

_____

<u>*Going Deeper:*</u>

In verse 5, we are told the invalid had been waiting at the pool for healing for *thirty-eight years!* The **NKJV MacArthur Study Bible, 2ⁿᵈ Edition** says regarding this number: *"John included this figure to emphasize the gravity of the debilitating disease that afflicted the individual. Since his sickness had been witnessed by many people for almost 4 decades, when Jesus cured him everyone knew the genuineness of the healing (cf. v. 9)."* **2**

_____

Devotion written by Pastor Frank & Samuel Gervasi

_____

1.   Ministry 127, https://ministry127.com/resources/illustration/the-importance-of-being-flexible, as accessed on 03/21/2025.
2.   Copyright © 1997, 2006, 2019 by Thomas Nelson. All rights reserved.

Going Deeper – A 30-Day Devotional

Going Deeper – A 30-Day Devotional

#29 - The Seeds We Are Planting
Read: *Philippians 1:1-11*

"It is right for me to feel this way about all of you, since I have you in my heart and, whether I am in chains or defending and confirming the gospel, all of you share in God's grace with me." ***Philippians 1:7, NIV***

When a boy came home from school one day, he found a neighbor's pickup truck backed up to his family's garden. Apparently, the boy's father had told the neighbor he could have the corn stalks for fodder. So, the young man got in the garden bed and helped pull the stalks out by the roots while he threw them into the truck bed. By the time they finished, the whole area looked like it had purposely been prepared for planting. So, the boy went and got a bag of peanuts that his grandmother had given him. He spaced them up and down the rows and ran out of peanuts right when he ran out of rows. Everything seemed perfect. However, it was not until *after* a thorough spanking by his father that it was made clear to him that the empty bed was not for the peanuts he had planted. The father had intended it for some other vegetable, but soon enough, that garden plot full of peanuts erupted into bloom. The yield produced an army cot piled high with peanuts to dry.

Big Idea: *Knowing Jesus and living for Him produces good fruit that glorifies God and builds others up.*

We may not be planting peanuts these days, but we are all planting seeds that produce fruit in the future. I heard one person say this: "That what we are on the

Going Deeper – A 30-Day Devotional

inside, will always show on the outside." The church at Philippi was commended by the Apostle Paul for the fruit their lives were producing, in two primary areas.

For one, he praised them for helping him share the Gospel with others, using the phrase *"...your partnership in the Gospel..."* in verse 5. I like that because it shows a mindset that realizes that a church grows when the **entire** church body takes the responsibility of bringing others the Good News. And if you think about it, they were faithful in doing this, because he also uses the phrase "from the beginning." Which implies that their faithfulness in sharing the Gospel was over an ample period.

———————————

Insight: **Living life in obedience to God's commands is the best way to create a lasting impact in this world. As believers, we naturally begin producing "the fruit of righteousness" because Christ lives in us. But we still often need to choose to obey God and live out our faith.**

———————————

The church at Philippi was also commended for their generosity. They were willing to use their financial resources that God had entrusted them for the furthering of God's work. The church at Philippi had previously sent gifts to the persecuted church in Jerusalem and had supported missionaries like Timothy and Epaphroditus. All these things showed their generosity.

The Apostle Paul responded to this fruit the church had demonstrated first by thanking God for them. Not just generally in passing, but "every time I remember you" (v. 3) and "for all of you." (v. 4) And finally, he prayed that *"...their love would abound more and more in knowledge and depth of insight..."* (v. 9) The church at Philippi had produced good fruit, but there was also room for growth. Even for us today, no matter how long we have been a Christian or how much we have grown in the past, none of us will arrive. We all need to continue growing and becoming more like Jesus. Paul was praying that Christ would continue working in their life. And in the end, they would bring glory to God, all because they were finding their identity in Him and producing the *"fruit of righteousness that comes through Jesus Christ to the glory and praise of God."* (v. 11)

"In Scripture the word 'seed' is used literally of the essential plant organism which enables the species to reproduce itself (Gen. 1:11)...It is also used in many

figurative ways: of human offspring, descendants, and progeny (Gen. 3:15, 13:15); of 'the word of the kingdom' (Mt. 13:3-23); of 'the children of the kingdom of heaven' (Mt. 13:38); of 'the word of God' (Lk. 8:11; 1 Pt. 1:23); and of 'the kingdom of heaven' itself (Mt. 13:31-32)." **1**

Challenge: **What fruit is my life producing? Does it bring glory and praise to God or not? How can I continue to grow in my walk with Christ?**

Pray: **Asking God to continue His good work in me, that I might bear fruit pleasing to Him...**

Going Deeper:

*In the Apostle Paul's prayer in verse 9, he prays that the Philippians' love would abound **"more and more"**. This phrase gives us a picture of one step on top of another and on top of another. Which shows us this: **sanctification is not always instantaneous**. Positionally, we are "sanctified" and washed clean the moment we accept Christ. But the actual "how-to" and application is a process. Sometimes it's 2 steps forward and 1 step back. Sometimes it's 1 step forward and 2 steps back! But we must remember that we are a work in progress. Christ is still working in our lives to make us more like Himself. Be comforted today that, "...he who began a good work in you will carry it on to completion until the day of Christ Jesus." (v. 6)*

Devotion written by Pastor Frank & Samuel Gervasi

---

1. Wycliffe Bible Dictionary, pg. 1543, Charles F. Pfeiffer, Howard F. Vos, John Rea

Going Deeper – A 30-Day Devotional

#30 - Who's the Person in the Mirror?
Read: *James 1:19-27*

"Anyone who listens to the word but does not do what it says is like someone who looks at his face in a mirror and, after looking at himself, goes away and immediately forgets what he looks like." James 1:23-24, NIV

Warren Wiersbe tells in his book *Be Free* the fact that young pastors and ministers often visited the great British preacher G. Campbell Morgan. They would often ask him the secret of his success. Because it was said that he had a genuine and solid Christian faith. Morgan was said to reply, *"I always say to them the same thing -- work; hard work; and again, work!"* **1** And Morgan lived up to his own advice. He would be in his study every morning at 6 o'clock, finding rich treasures out of his Bible to pass on to God's people.

Big Idea: *Practicing biblical commands is for all believers and should be practiced so each person can grow, avoiding hypocrisy.*

God wants us to strive for growth always practicing biblical principles and applying them to our lives. *"Brothers and sisters" (v. 19)* were terms that were reserved for Christ-followers. Sometimes people want to say that God will grow us as we pursue Him. And that's true but that should never be used as an excuse to NOT try, push, strive, and deliberately attempt to grow into a mature believer in Jesus Christ, especially areas that we can. Now, of course the areas that are difficult for us specifically, will require God's help through the Holy Spirit and prayer.

Going Deeper – A 30-Day Devotional

James lists several different areas that a mature life is shown. For instance, being a good listener *"Everyone should be quick to listen and slow to speak." (v. 19.)* He also lists controlling our temper, *"slow to become angry." (v. 19.)* As well as avoiding wicked behavior *"Therefore get rid of all moral filth and the evil that is so prevalent" (v. 21.)* All ways are characteristic of a person who is mature in faith.

———————

Insight: *Learning God's commands should be learned and applied always, so we can experience God's best. We should also avoid the mindsets that hinder our walk of faith.*

———————

The reasons can be many for why we don't experience God's best in life. Sometimes the mindsets can be *felt like we can't grow* anymore or *not realizing when we don't* because of personal ignorance. Other times it may be *tiring to do good* when so many around us can be doing the opposite. Regardless of why though we can be sure God doesn't want us to deliberately avoid holiness and outwardly show others something different. Hypocrisy was always discouraged by Christ. James's style of writing was considered *in your face by some.* However, it may have been because he wanted Christians to practice what they were learning. Which could be seen in several ways in everyday interactions. He challenges others whether they were living out their faith in tangible ways like speech (v. 26,) helping the less fortunate (v. 27,) and maintaining a proper focus (v. 27) when he says *"to keep oneself from being polluted by the World.:"*

A popular statement regarding how a Christian can reconcile the differences in how we should live biblically, and the culture around us is: *Be in the World but Not of it!*

———————

Challenge: *What do I see when I look at myself? Does my life align with how the Scriptures teach me or not? How can I continue to grow in faith?*

Pray: *Asking God to continue His work in the areas of my life, so my faith is being lived out....*

———————

Going Deeper:

Ancient biblical writers sometimes paralleled growth with everyday objects that people were familiar with. However, his use or comparison with a man looking in the mirror and forgetting what they looked like was a powerful one. The *NIV Cultural Backgrounds Study Bible* says, *"Some moral teachers recommended use of a mirror for moral reflection. Ancient mirrors rarely produced the more accurate images available today."* **2** If that is true about the quality of mirrors in bible times, then James is possibly showing the lack of commitment to remembering biblical commands enough to apply them. We can assume that if we are to grow in faith, it will take effort on our part to be successful.

Devotion written by Pastor Frank & Samuel Gervasi

1.   Be Free, Chariot Victor Publishing, Copyright 1975.
2.   NIV Cultural Backgrounds Study Bible, Zondervan, Copyright 2016

Going Deeper – A 30-Day Devotional

www.ingramcontent.com/pod-product-compliance
Lightning Source LLC
Chambersburg PA
CBHW071324130626
46556CB00004B/1742